Teacher's Guide
to the handbook

. . . a teacher's guide to accompany

WRITE SOURCE

GREAT SOURCE EDUCATION GROUP

a division of Houghton Mifflin Company
Boston, Massachusetts

About the Teacher's Guide

Write on Track

It's important for you to know a few things about your *Write on Track Teacher's Guide* before you begin to use it.

Previewing ● The opening section provides a quick tour of the handbook to help you become familiar with its basic features. The next section—"Getting Started Activities"—contains guidelines and reproducible activity sheets that you can use to introduce the handbook to your students.

Planning ● "Using *Write on Track* in the Classroom" provides a variety of ideas for planning instruction. The next three sections contain summaries for all of the handbook chapters related to writing and learning skills. The "Handbook Minilessons" section contains a variety of activities to use along with the handbook. (At least one minilesson is provided for each handbook chapter.)

Managing ● "Evaluating/Assessing/Monitoring" offers suggestions for evaluating writing, basic-skills instruction, and extended units. Also included in this section is valuable information related to peer conferencing and portfolio assessment.

Supplementing ● The final sections in the *Teacher's Guide* serve as a resource for improving instruction with the handbook. "Reading-Writing Connection" lists high-interest trade books related to major chapters in the handbook. These lists can help when planning extended units. The "Bibliography" section lists additional resources for each chapter, which may also help during planning. Finally, "Program Overview" highlights the coordinating program for grade 3.

Authors: Dave Kemper, Ruth Nathan, and Patrick Sebranek

Printed in the United States of America

International Standard Book Number: 0-669-40882-4

1 2 3 4 5 6 7 8 9 10 -DBH- 01 00 99 98 97 96

What You'll Find Inside

A
QUICK Tour

Write on Track Student Handbook

Write on Track serves as the perfect language handbook for grade 3, one that will help your students improve their ability **to write** (prewriting through proofreading), **to think** (creatively, logically, and clearly), and **to learn** (in the classroom, in small groups, independently). This quick tour will highlight the handbook's major points of interest.

The Process of Writing

Students will use this section of the handbook to answer their questions about writing, from selecting a subject to proofreading a final draft.

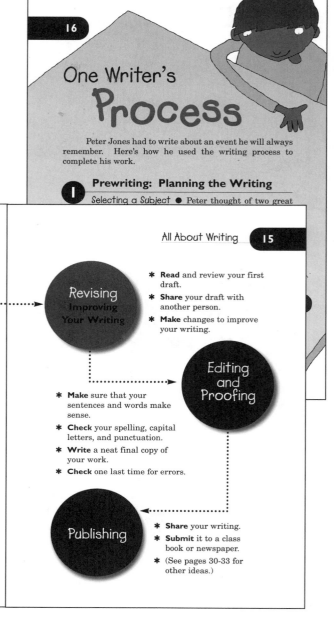

16

One Writer's Process

Peter Jones had to write about an event he will always remember. Here's how he used the writing process to complete his work.

1 Prewriting: Planning the Writing

Selecting a Subject ● Peter thought of two great

14

The Writing Process in Action

Writers like Emily use the **writing process**. The steps in the writing process are listed on the next two pages. You should follow these steps when you write your own stories, reports, and other things. The writing process will help you do your best work—just like it helps Emily and other writers!

The Writing Process

Prewriting

* **Select** a subject.
* **Collect** details about your subject.

Revising
Improving Your Writing

* **Read** and review your first draft.
* **Share** your draft with another person.
* **Make** changes to improve your writing.

Editing and Proofing

* **Make** sure that your sentences and words make sense.
* **Check** your spelling, capital letters, and punctuation.
* **Write** a neat final copy of your work.
* **Check** one last time for errors.

Publishing

* **Share** your writing.
* **Submit** it to a class book or newspaper.
* (See pages 30-33 for other ideas.)

Revising Checklist

Do I need to **add** any information?
- [ ] Do I have a good beginning?
- [ ] Have I included all the important details?
- [ ] Do I need to add an ending?

Do I need to **cut** any information?
- [ ] Have I stuck to my topic?
- [ ] Have I repeated myself in some parts?

Do I need to **move** any parts?
- [ ] Are my sentences in the best order?
- [ ] Do any ideas or details seem to be out of place?

Do I need to **rewrite** any parts?
- [ ] Are there ideas or sentences that are unclear?
- [ ] Have I used my five senses?

Colorful illustrations and a personal tone are used throughout *Write on Track*. Step-by-step instructions, helpful guidelines, and checklists make information easy to find and use.

2 The Forms of Writing

When students are ready to start a personal journal, write a poem, or create a time-travel fantasy, this is the section to turn to.

152

Writing Photo Essays

Have you ever opened a book with photos and said, "Cool!" We have, too. Photos can show you what words can only tell you. They make learning more real and exciting.

The "Show and Tell" of Writing

Photo essays share information or tell stories using words and photos. For example, in *Rosie, A Visiting Dog's Story,* by Stephanie Calmenson, the ... how a dog cheers up sick children. The ... Rosie at work in a hospital. ... chapter, we'll show you part of a photo ... ents just like you. Then we'll tell you ... your own.

144

Writing Classroom Reports

100% FAT FREE
NO PEANUT
PEANUT BUTTER

The world is full of things to care about: dolphins, spiders, volcanoes, tornadoes, space, holidays, peanuts. (Yes, peanuts. J... without pe... get to shar... about a sub...

Getting Started

Andy Levin liked ... knew something about t... out even more when ... chapter will show you w... classroom report. Then ...

178

Making Friends with a Poem

Once you start writing poems, you will probably enjoy reading a lot of them, too. When you read poems, you learn how they look and sound. Follow these steps to make friends with each new poem you read.

▶ **Read the poem to yourself two or three times.**

▶ **Read it out loud. (Listen to what it says.)**

▶ **Share the poem with a friend. (Talk about it.)**

▶ **Copy the poem in a special notebook.**

Now make friends with this poem written by a student like you!

Elephant Poem

Rumbling
　Rumbling
Rumbling
12,000 pounds are coming.
Crashing,
bashing,
trashing,　mashing,
dashing,　gnashing,
on
　leaves.
Elephant noises all around.
　　　—Claudia Mark

Write on Track **addresses many forms of writing, from explanations to plays.**

If your students' study, reading, or test-taking skills could use a little pumping up, have them turn to "The Tools of Learning."

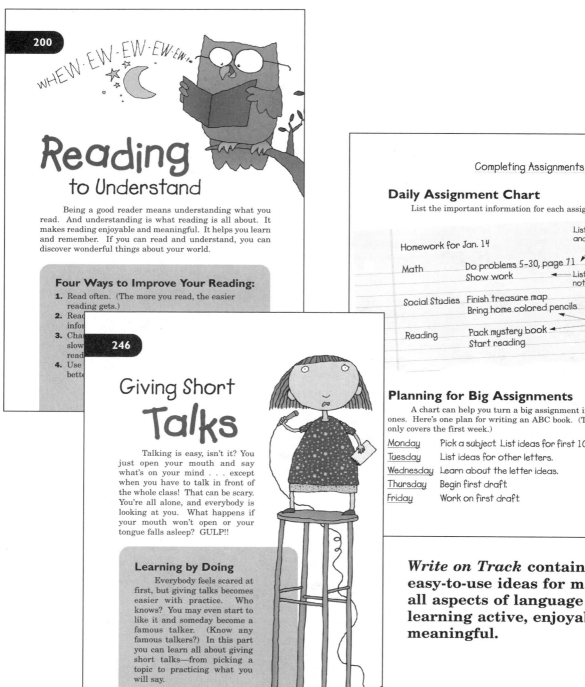

200

WHEW-EW-EW-EW-EW-EW-EW-!~

Reading
to Understand

Being a good reader means understanding what you read. And understanding is what reading is all about. It makes reading enjoyable and meaningful. It helps you learn and remember. If you can read and understand, you can discover wonderful things about your world.

Four Ways to Improve Your Reading:
1. Read often. (The more you read, the easier reading gets.)
2. Read
   infor
3. Cha
   slow
   read
4. Use
   bette

246

Giving Short
Talks

Talking is easy, isn't it? You just open your mouth and say what's on your mind . . . except when you have to talk in front of the whole class! That can be scary. You're all alone, and everybody is looking at you. What happens if your mouth won't open or your tongue falls asleep? GULP!!

Learning by Doing
Everybody feels scared at first, but giving talks becomes easier with practice. Who knows? You may even start to like it and someday become a famous talker. (Know any famous talkers?) In this part you can learn all about giving short talks—from picking a topic to practicing what you will say.

Completing Assignments **279**

Daily Assignment Chart
List the important information for each assignment.

Homework for Jan. 14

Math   Do problems 5-30, page 71   ← List pages and numbers.
              Show work   ← List special notes.

Social Studies Finish treasure map
                Bring home colored pencils
                                            ← List supplies.
Reading   Pack mystery book
              Start reading

Planning for Big Assignments
A chart can help you turn a big assignment into little ones. Here's one plan for writing an ABC book. (This plan only covers the first week.)

Monday	Pick a subject. List ideas for first 10 letters.
Tuesday	List ideas for other letters.
Wednesday	Learn about the letter ideas.
Thursday	Begin first draft.
Friday	Work on first draft.

***Write on Track* contains lots of easy-to-use ideas for making all aspects of language and learning active, enjoyable, and meaningful.**

Whenever students have a question about punctuation, spelling, or capitalization, they can turn to the yellow pages for help.

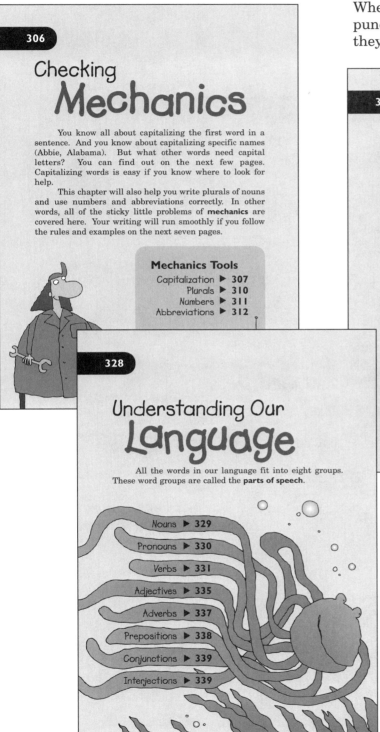

306

Checking Mechanics

You know all about capitalizing the first word in a sentence. And you know about capitalizing specific names (Abbie, Alabama). But what other words need capital letters? You can find out on the next few pages. Capitalizing words is easy if you know where to look for help.

This chapter will also help you write plurals of nouns and use numbers and abbreviations correctly. In other words, all of the sticky little problems of **mechanics** are covered here. Your writing will run smoothly if you follow the rules and examples on the next seven pages.

328

Understanding Our Language

All the words in our language fit into eight groups. These word groups are called the **parts of speech**.

318

Using the Right Word

This chapter lists common homophones (*say* `hä-mə-fōnz*). Homophones are words that sound the same but have different spellings or meanings like *to, too,* and *two*. If you know the common homophones, you won't make a mistake like this in your writing:

I *blue* my nose.

Sounds like someone painted his or her nose, doesn't it? *Blew* is the right word to use.

ant, aunt	Ants are insects that work hard. It's a blast when my aunt baby-sits for us.
ate, eight	I ate the teacher's apple. My friend had eight pieces of licorice.
bare, bear	She tested the water with her bare feet. Watch for bears when you pick berries.

This guide to spelling, usage, punctuation, and capitalization answers all your students' proofreading questions.

5 The Student Almanac

Full-color maps, a historical time line, the metric system—*Write on Track* is truly an all-school handbook!

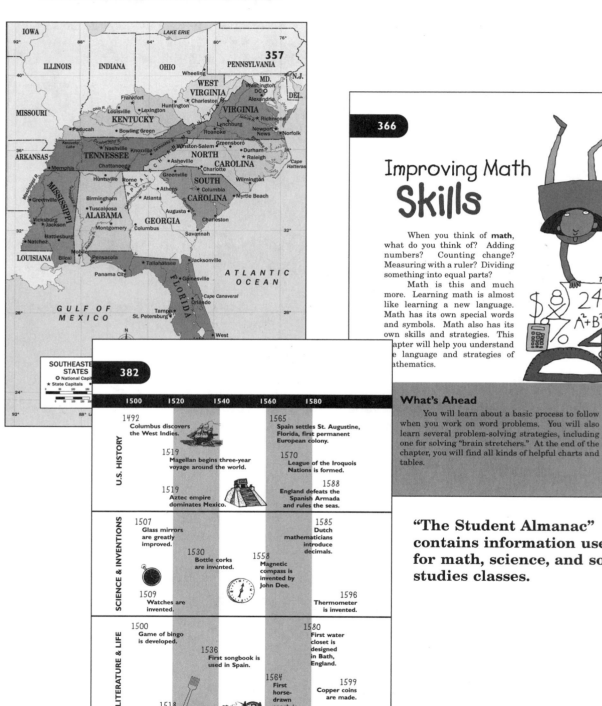

Improving Math Skills

When you think of **math**, what do you think of? Adding numbers? Counting change? Measuring with a ruler? Dividing something into equal parts?

Math is this and much more. Learning math is almost like learning a new language. Math has its own special words and symbols. Math also has its own skills and strategies. This chapter will help you understand the language and strategies of mathematics.

What's Ahead

You will learn about a basic process to follow when you work on word problems. You will also learn several problem-solving strategies, including one for solving "brain stretchers." At the end of the chapter, you will find all kinds of helpful charts and tables.

"The Student Almanac" contains information useful for math, science, and social studies classes.

Getting Started

ACTIVITIES

Write on Track was developed by experienced teachers and writers for students in third grade and beyond. More than anything else, we wanted to put together a handbook that students would find very helpful *and* very enjoyable to use. Over the past several years, teachers have told us what they like best about our other handbooks, and what they do when the book is first put into the hands of their students.

Learning About the Handbook

Many of their suggestions, plus some of our own, are contained in this section of your *Teacher's Guide*. Of special interest to you will be the suggested sequences of activities (page 11) for introducing the handbook to your students and the reproducible activity sheets on pages 12-18.

Start-Up Ideas

*Use the ideas listed on the next two pages to help
your students learn about and use* Write on Track.

Scavenger Hunts

Create scavenger hunts asking students to find facts or ideas listed in the handbook. Scavenger hunts can be implemented individually in daily language practice activities or in extended activities, in which you provide students with a series of questions to answer. (See "Reproducible Activities" below for extended activities.)

Example Scavenger Hunts:

Easy ✶ Turn to page 21. Does the mouse on the page squeak? _____

More Challenging ✶ Turn to the index. On what page would you learn how to capitalize days and months? _____

A Definite Challenge ✶ On what page would you learn how to make your own book? _____ How many steps does it take? _____

Reproducible Activities

Implement the activity sheets provided for you on pages 12-18 in this section. Select only those activities that meet the needs and the nature of your students. Many of the activities can be done by students working in pairs.

One Point of Interest

Give your students the following assignment: Find one page, checklist, chart, illustration, or model that you really like or that you think is really important. (Students should be prepared to share their discoveries with a small group of classmates or with the entire class.)

Five W's

Provide small groups of students (2 or 3 individuals) with *who, what, when, where,* and *why* questions from *Write on Track.* Then have each group find and record answers to these questions. (This activity could be turned into a contest or game.)

Example questions:

Who writes lists?

What is the last step in the writing process?

A Variation: Small groups of students could develop 5-W's questions for the class to answer.

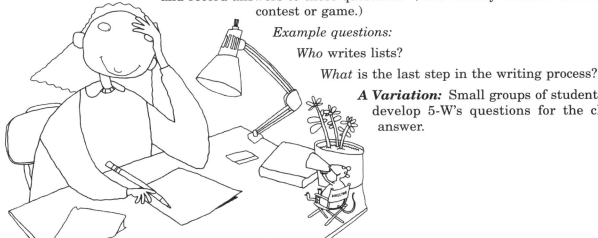

Wall Charts

Have small groups of students design wall charts based on helpful checklists or guidelines contained in *Write on Track*. (The "Conference Checklist" on page 51 is an example.) Display the finished products in the classroom as well as in other rooms in the school.

Sharing Sessions

Reserve time on Fridays to have students share positive experiences using the handbook: "I found the words *to, too,* and *two* in the handbook. After reading about these words, I now know how to use them." Sharing sessions will help students appreciate *Write on Track* as a valuable resource.

Minilessons

Conduct minilessons on a regular basis to give your students practice using *Write on Track*. We think of minilessons as activities that can be completed in 10-15 minutes.

Example Minilessons:

Bests, Worsts, and Favorites .... *Building a File of Writing Ideas*

MAKE three columns in your writing notebook. **WRITE** one of these words at the top of each column: *Bests, Worsts, Favorites.* **LIST** writing ideas under each column. (To help you get started, see the top of page 37 in the handbook.)

Wheels of Words .... *Describing a Subject*

DRAW a describing wheel on a piece of paper. (See page 265 in the handbook for an example.) **NAME** a favorite personal object in the middle of your wheel. Then **LIST** describing words on the spokes around your subject. **SHARE** your work.

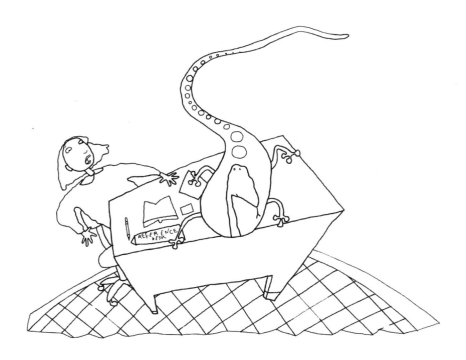

Your First Week with the Handbook

DAY 1

Distribute copies of *Write on Track* and give your students a few minutes to preview the handbook. Have them share first impressions. Then discuss how the handbook is organized, referring students to the introductory page (page 3), the table of contents (pages 4-7), and the index (pages 392-400).

To help students get to know the handbook, ask them to work on one of the reproducible activity sheets. We recommend that you implement "About the Handbook: I or II" (pages 12 and 13 in this section).

DAY 2

Provide time at the beginning of the class period for students to complete their work on the activity sheet. Then discuss the results. (See the answer key on pages 19-26 in this section of your guide.)

For the rest of the class period, ask students to complete the "One Point of Interest" activity described on page 3 in this section.

DAY 3

Have students share their points of interest in small groups or with the entire class.

To help students understand that *Write on Track* is an all-school handbook, have them complete the "Your All-School Handbook" activity sheet (page 14).

DAY 4

Have students share the results of their work using the NEXT STOP at the bottom of the "All-School" activity sheet.

Read "Why Write?" (pages 8-9 in *Write on Track)* aloud. Stress the fact that students should keep their handbook next to them when they write *and* when they study.

With any time remaining, have students work on one of the reproducible activity sheets or on one of the other start-up ideas.

DAY 5

Discuss the students' work on the activity from the previous day.

Have small groups of students (2 or 3 individuals) work on 5-W's questions that can be used periodically in classroom activities. (See page 9 in this section for examples.)

SPECIAL NOTE

Continue reading, sharing, and learning about different parts of the handbook from week to week throughout the school year.

About the Handbook: I

DIRECTIONS: Turn to the table of contents in your handbook. Write down the page number that would help you answer each question below.

 How do you write with a *computer*? _____

 What does *conferencing* mean? _____

 What does a *business letter* look like? _____

 How do you *tell a story* out loud? _____

 Why are *punctuation marks* important? _____

DIRECTIONS: Now turn to the index. Write down a page number that would help you answer each question below.

 What is an *adverb*? _____

 How do you write a *cinquain poem*? _____

 How do you fold a *letter*? _____

 What does the *plot* of a story mean? _____

 Is a *Venn diagram* hard to use? _____

About the Handbook: II

DIRECTIONS: Turn to the table of contents in your handbook. Write down the page number that would help you answer each question below.

 Are there many ways to *publish* writing? _____

2 When would you write a *summary*? _____

3 How do you write a *photo essay*? _____

 When is it important to *work in groups*? _____

5 How can you improve your *handwriting*? _____

DIRECTIONS: Now turn to the index. Write down a page number that would help you answer each question below.

 What is a *biography*? _____

 When would you use a *gathering grid*? _____

 How do you correct a *run-on sentence*? _____

 What is the *theme* of a story? _____

 When would you use *your* instead of *you're*? _____

Your All-School Handbook

Write on Track can help you in *all* of your subjects.

DIRECTIONS: List two chapters from the handbook that can help you in four different subjects. One space has been filled in to get you started.

Writing
Building a File of Writing Ideas, 35-37

Reading

Social Studies

Math

When you finish, share your work with your classmates. Give a reason for each one of your choices.

Staying on Track

DIRECTIONS: To complete this chart, find words from five different lists in *Write on Track*. The lists are named along the top of the chart. Each word must begin with one of the letters in the lefthand column. (Two words have been filled in for you.)

	Dictionary of Prefixes, Suffixes, and Roots	English from Around the World*	Using the Right Word	Checking Your Spelling	State Abbreviations
O					
N	negative				
T					
R	rosy				
A					
C					
K					

* You can find this list in the chapter "A History of the English Language."

Handbook Training

DIRECTIONS: Answer each question in the trains below.

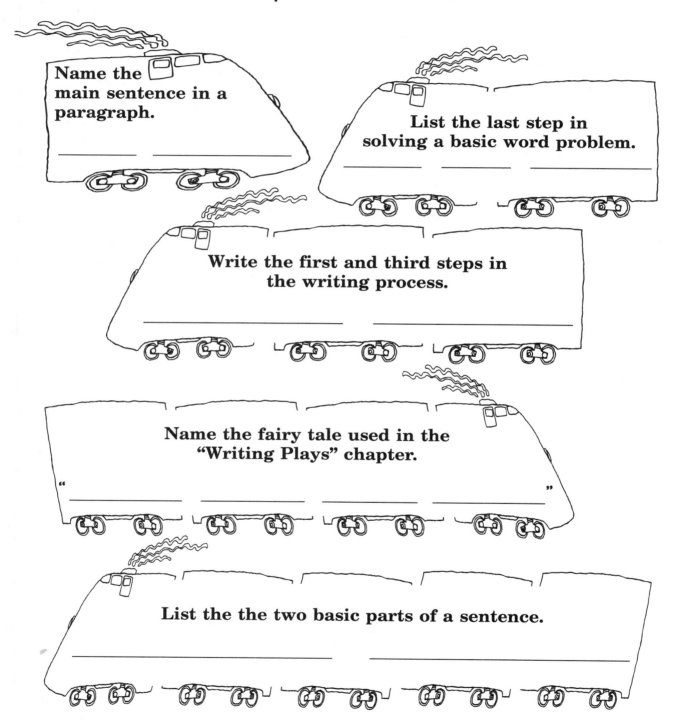

Name the main sentence in a paragraph.

List the last step in solving a basic word problem.

Write the first and third steps in the writing process.

Name the fairy tale used in the "Writing Plays" chapter.

"_____"

List the the two basic parts of a sentence.

Whistle-stops in **Write on Track**

**DIRECTIONS: Use your handbook to find the information for each stop
listed below. The first one has been done for you.**

 page 93
The name of the girl who
wrote a friendly letter

 A N D R E A

 page 84
The first food
on the list

___ ___ ___ ___ ___ ___

 page 227
The plural of the word
donkey

___ ___ ___ ___ ___ ___ ___

 page 321
The homophone for *write*

___ ___ ___ ___ ___

 page 105
Another name for an
ABC book

___ ___ ___ ___ ___ ___ ___ ___ ___

 page 69
The name of a green
vegetable

___ ___ ___ ___ ___ ___ ___ ___ ___

 page 345
The name for a female
lion

___ ___ ___ ___ ___ ___ ___

 page 389
The last name of a famous
pilot

___ ___ ___ ___ ___ ___ ___ ___ ___

 page 168
The last word on the page

___ ___ ___ ___

 NEXT STOP

Write the first letter of each answer.

___ ___ ___ ___ ___ ___ ___ ___

Unscramble the letters to find a two-word message.
Hint: It's about getting on a train.

___ ___ ___ ___ ___ ___ ___ ___ ___!

Write on Track Facts

DIRECTIONS: Fifteen statements are listed below. Check each statement in the handbook to see if it is true or false. (The first one has been done for you.)

		True	**False**
1	There are 382 pages in *Write on Track*.		X
2	The illustrator of *Write on Track* is Chris Krenzke.		
3	The table of contents starts on page 4.		
4	There are three main steps in the Writing Process.		
5	"Conferencing" means working by yourself.		
6	The pages in the "Proofreader's Guide" are yellow.		
7	A comma is used in numbers of four or more digits.		
8	A moral is an invented or made-up story.		
9	KWL is a reading strategy.		
10	Prefixes are word parts that come at the end of a word.		
11	Bandwagon is a selling method used in commercials.		
12	Friendly letters and business letters look exactly alike.		
13	There are two poetry chapters in *Write on Track*.		
14	The very first date in the historical time line is 1600.		
15	*Write on Track* has a math chart for skip-counting.		

Getting Started

ACTIVITIES

ANSWER KEY

About the Handbook: I

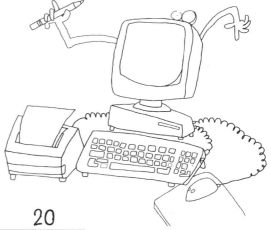

DIRECTIONS: Turn to the table of contents in your handbook. Write down the page number that would help you answer each question below.

 How do you write with a *computer*? ____20____

 What does *conferencing* mean? ____48____

 What does a *business letter* look like? ____122____

 How do you *tell a story* out loud? ____256____

 Why are *punctuation marks* important? ____295____

DIRECTIONS: Now turn to the index. Write down a page number that would help you answer each question below.

6 What is an *adverb*? ____337____

7 How do you write a *cinquain poem*? ____185____

8 How do you fold a *letter*? ____129____

9 What does the *plot* of a story mean? ____121____

10 Is a *Venn diagram* hard to use? ____266____

Name _____

About the Handbook: II

DIRECTIONS: Turn to the table of contents in your handbook. Write down the page number that would help you answer each question below.

 Are there many ways to *publish* writing? _____30_____

 When would you write a *summary*? _____64_____

 How do you write a *photo essay*? _____152_____

 When is it important to *work in groups*? _____280_____

 How can you improve your *handwriting*? _____376_____

DIRECTIONS: Now turn to the index. Write down a page number that would help you answer each question below.

 What is a *biography*? _____121_____

 When would you use a *gathering grid*? _____148_____

 How do you correct a *run-on sentence*? _____71_____

 What is the *theme* of a story? _____121_____

 When would you use *your* instead of *you're*? _____323_____

Your All-School Handbook

Write on Track can help you in *all* of your subjects.

DIRECTIONS: List two chapters from the handbook that can help you in four different subjects. One space has been filled in to get you started.

Writing
Building a File of Writing Ideas, 35-37

Reading

(Answers will vary.)

Social Studies

Math

When you finish, share your work with your classmates. Give a reason for each one of your choices.

Staying on Track

DIRECTIONS: To complete this chart, find words from five different lists in *Write on Track*. The lists are named along the top of the chart. Each word must begin with one of the letters in the lefthand column. (Two words have been filled in for you.)

	Dictionary of Prefixes, Suffixes, and Roots	English from Around the World*	Using the Right Word	Checking Your Spelling	State Abbreviations
O					
N	negative				
T					
R	rosy		(Answers will vary.)		
A					
C					
K					

* You can find this list in the chapter "A History of the English Language."

Handbook Training

DIRECTIONS: Answer each question in the trains below.

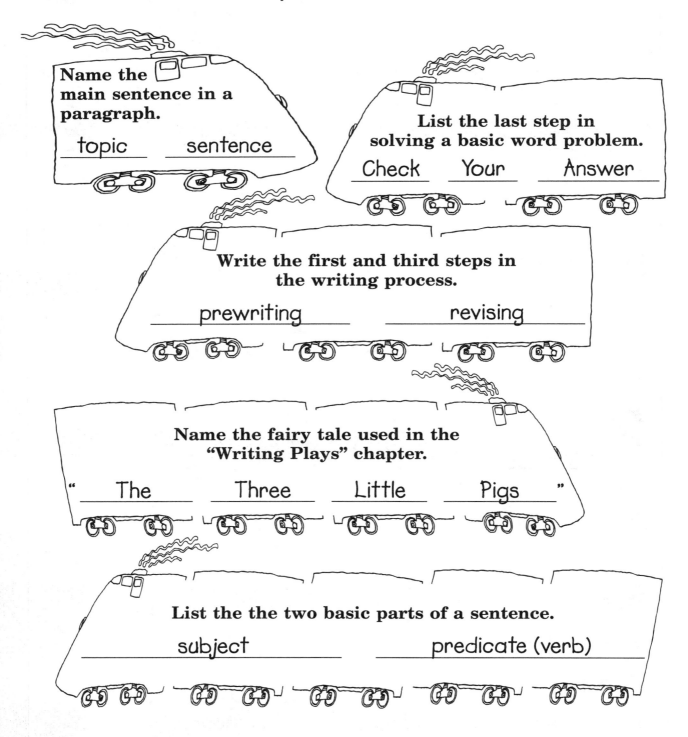

Name the main sentence in a paragraph.

topic   sentence

List the last step in solving a basic word problem.

Check   Your   Answer

Write the first and third steps in the writing process.

prewriting   revising

Name the fairy tale used in the "Writing Plays" chapter.

" The   Three   Little   Pigs "

List the the two basic parts of a sentence.

subject   predicate (verb)

Whistle-stops in **Write on Track**

DIRECTIONS: Use your handbook to find the information for each stop listed below. The first one has been done for you.

 page 93
The name of the girl who wrote a friendly letter

<u>A N D R E A</u>

 page 69
The name of a green vegetable

<u>B R O C C O L I</u>

 page 84
The first food on the list

<u>A L F A L F A</u>

 page 345
The name for a female lion

<u>L I O N E S S</u>

 page 227
The plural of the word donkey

<u>D O N K E Y S</u>

 page 389
The last name of a famous pilot

<u>L I N D B E R G H</u>

 page 321
The homophone for *write*

<u>R I G H T</u>

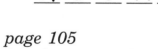 *page 168*
The last word on the page

<u>O U T</u>

 *page 105*
Another name for an ABC book

<u>A L P H A B E T</u>   <u>B O O K</u>

Write the first letter of each answer.

<u>A A D R A B L L O</u>

Unscramble the letters to find a two-word message.
Hint: It's about getting on a train.

<u>A L L</u>   <u>A B O A R D</u>!

Write on Track Facts

DIRECTIONS: Fifteen statements are listed below. Check each statement in the handbook to see if it is true or false. (The first one has been done for you.)

		True	False
1	There are 382 pages in *Write on Track*.		X
2	The illustrator of *Write on Track* is Chris Krenzke.	X	
3	The table of contents starts on page 4.	X	
4	There are three main steps in the Writing Process.		X
5	"Conferencing" means working by yourself.		X
6	The pages in the "Proofreader's Guide" are yellow.	X	
7	A comma is used in numbers of four or more digits.	X	
8	A moral is an invented or made-up story.		X
9	KWL is a reading strategy.	X	
10	Prefixes are word parts that come at the end of a word.		X
11	Bandwagon is a selling method used in commercials.	X	
12	Friendly letters and business letters look exactly alike.		X
13	There are two poetry chapters in *Write on Track*.	X	
14	The very first date in the historical time line is 1600.		X
15	*Write on Track* has a math chart for skip-counting.	X	

Using *Write on Track*

in the CLASSROOM

Teachers often ask how *Write on Track* can be used in their classrooms. The answer to that question is easy. Teachers should think of *Write on Track* as their teacher's aide, on hand to help students at all times—during class, throughout the school day, and later at home—with their writing, reading, and learning. The following pages provide ideas for making the handbook work in the classroom.

Where **Write on Track** Fits In

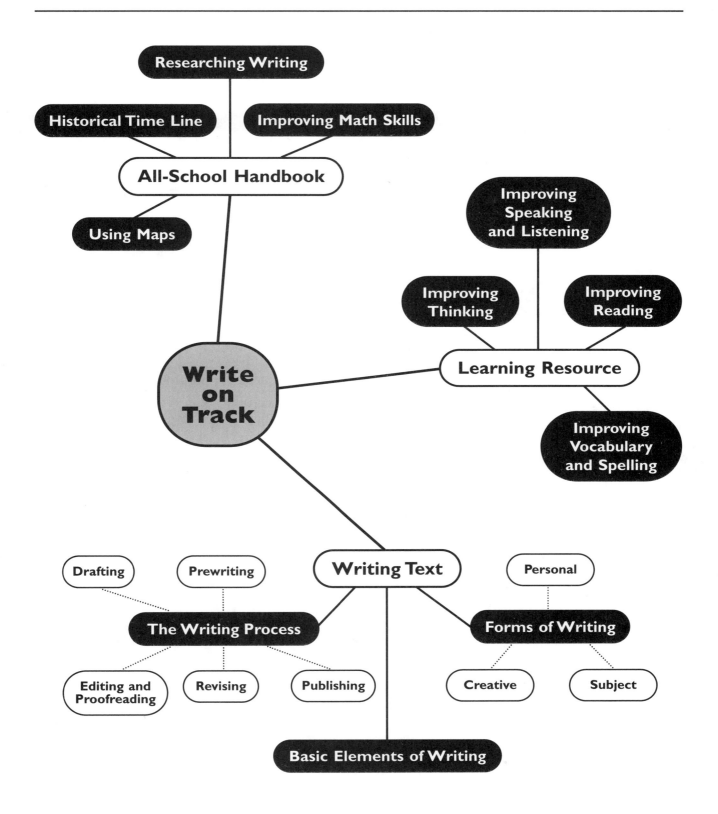

Framework of Writing Activities

The types of writing in *Write on Track* are listed below in a possible framework or sequence of activities, moving from personal writing to writing that becomes more inventive and reflective. Teachers can use this framework as a starting point when planning a writing program with the handbook.

PERSONAL WRITING	
Recording	Writing in Journals (p. 77) Writing to Learn Math (p. 274) Reading to Understand: Mapping (p. 204)
Recalling and Remembering	Writing Paragraphs: Narrative Paragraph (p. 58) Making Albums (p. 82) Writing Personal Narratives (p. 96)
SUBJECT WRITING	
Introducing	Writing Family Stories (p. 100)
Describing	Writing Paragraphs: Descriptive Paragraph (p. 59)
Reporting	Writing Newspaper Stories (p. 110)
Corresponding	Writing Friendly Notes (p. 88) Writing Friendly Letters (p. 92) Writing Business Letters: Asking for Information (p. 125)
Informing	Writing Paragraphs: Expository Paragraph (p. 60) Writing to Explain (p. 130) Writing Photo Essays (p. 152)
Searching and Researching	Writing Alphabet Books (p. 105) Writing a Summary (p. 64) Writing Classroom Reports (p. 144)
CREATIVE WRITING	
Imagining	Writing Realistic Stories (p. 159) Writing Time-Travel Fantasies (p. 164)
Inventing	Writing Lists (p. 84) Writing Plays (p. 170) Writing Free-Verse Poetry (p. 177) Writing Other Forms of Poetry (p. 184)
REFLECTIVE WRITING	
Applying and Analyzing	Writing Business Letters: Solving a Problem (p. 128)
Persuading	Writing Paragraphs: Persuasive Paragraph (p. 61) Writing Newspaper Stories: Letter to the Editor (p. 115)
Reviewing	Writing Book Reviews (p. 116)

Yearlong Timetable

The next four pages provide a suggested yearlong timetable of writing activities using *Write on Track*. Adjust the timetable to meet the needs of your students and the nature of your classroom.

Week	Writing Activities	Rationale
1	**Introducing the Handbook**	See the "Getting Started Activities" section in the Teacher's Guide for this introduction.
2	**All About Writing** **One Writer's Process**	These two chapters reinforce the idea that writing is a process.
3	**Writing Personal Narratives** **Conferencing with Partners**	Teaching children how to conference is done within the context of narrative writing.
4	**Writing Personal Narratives** *(cont.)* **Revising Your Writing** **Editing and Proofreading**	Personal narrative work is extended to reinforce the process approach to writing.
5	**Building a File of Writing Ideas** **Writing Lists**	A file of writing ideas is an important addition to the students' writing folders. Ideas from this file can be used in "Writing Lists."
6	**Writing Friendly Notes**	This form of writing encourages the use of classroom mailboxes.
7	**Collecting Details** **Planning and Drafting Guide**	"Collecting Details" and "Planning and Drafting Guide" address important prewriting and writing strategies.
8-9	**Writing Paragraphs**	Students will be ready for this important type of writing by the end of the quarter.

Special Note: Use chapters in "The Tools of Learning" and basic-skills information in "The Proofreader's Guide" to enrich your students' writing and learning during the quarter.

Yearlong Timetable

Week	Writing Activities	Rationale
1	**Writing Basic Sentences** **Combining Sentences**	These chapters address two basic elements of writing: sentence correctness and sentence style.
2	**Writing Book Reviews**	Writing book reviews introduces students to analytical writing.
3	**Writing Free-Verse Poetry**	Students are thinking free-verse poems all of the time. This chapter helps them capture these poems on paper.
4	**Planning Portfolios**	Introduce students to personal or classroom portfolios now that they have completed a number of finished drafts.
5	**Publishing Your Writing**	At this point in the year, exploring different publishing possibilities is in order.
6-7	**Writing Family Stories**	Family stories are perfect for holiday gift giving.
8-9	**Writing Friendly Letters** **Writing Other Forms of Poetry**	Students should be encouraged to write friendly letters during the holiday or semester break. Working with traditional poetry forms is a nice way to end the semester.

Special Note: Use chapters in "The Tools of Learning" and basic-skills information in "The Proofreader's Guide" to enrich your students' writing and learning during the quarter.

Yearlong Timetable

Week	Writing Activities	Rationale
1	**Making Albums**	This is the perfect chapter in which to capture vacation-break highlights.
2	**Writing Newspaper Stories**	With the energy that comes after vacation, this is a good time to introduce news stories.
3-4	**Writing Alphabet Books**	Alphabet books require steadfast determination. Most third graders will enjoy the challenge. (Author teams work well!)
5	**Writing a Summary**	Summaries will be used often when students work on interviewing and when they develop photo essays or classroom reports.
6	**Writing Business Letters**	This form of writing connects students to the real world. They can, among other things, ask for information in business letters.
7-9	**Writing Photo Essays** *or* **Writing Classroom Reports**	When students write photo essays or reports, they learn about basic research skills: exploring a subject or question, gathering information, organizing facts and details, and so on.

Special Note: Use chapters in "The Tools of Learning" and basic-skills information in "The Proofreader's Guide" to enrich your students' writing and learning during the quarter.

Yearlong Timetable

Week	Writing Activities	Rationale
1-2	**Writing to Explain** **Giving Short Talks**	After writing to explain how to do or make different things, students will be ready to give short talks.
3-5	**Writing Realistic Stories** *or* **Writing Time-Travel Fantasies**	Either form of fiction offers students an exciting opportunity to be creative and inventive.
6-8	**Writing Plays**	This is a wonderful end-of-the-year activity that will engage all aspects of your students' learning—reading, writing, speaking, and listening. It will also encourage the writing of plays all summer long. Plays can be performed using traditional methods or reader's theater.
9	**Wrap-Up**	It's time to celebrate students' portfolios.

Special Note: Use chapters in "The Tools of Learning" and basic-skills information in "The Proofreader's Guide" to enrich your students' writing and learning during the quarter.

A Week with the Handbook

Here's how one week from the Yearlong Timetable could be implemented. (This is week 3 in the first quarter.)

DAY

1 Large-Group Activity

Introduce the personal narrative using handbook pages 96 and 97. Then model the prewriting activities "List Topic Ideas" and "Select One Idea" on page 98. Use the lives of well-known characters (like Goldilocks or Ramona Quimby) for these activities.

2 Individual Activity

Have students work on the prewriting activities on page 98.

Large-Group Activity

During the second part of the period, introduce "Plan Your Writing" on page 98.

3 Individual Activity

Instruct students with completed plans to begin working on their first drafts. Encourage them to use page 99 to help them with their drafting.

Teacher-Guided Guide any students who need planning and drafting help. Some students may benefit from telling their stories orally or drawing pictures before they begin drafting.

4 Individual Activity

Instruct students to continue working on their first drafts.

Large-Group Activity

Introduce students to the chapter "Conferencing with Partners" on pages 48-51. Role-play (with the help of another teacher, an aide, or a student) two writers involved in a conference.

5 Individual Activity

Have students complete their first drafts and carry out a peer conference with a writing partner. Instruct them to make a copy of the "Memorable/More" response sheet on page 51 to use during their conference.

Teacher-Guided Conduct a small-group conference with students who need more direct help.

During the next week students will complete their narratives. Revision and editing and proofreading will also be introduced.

Complementary Chapters:

Collecting Details (pages 38-39)   Telling Stories (pages 256-261)
Writing in Journals (pages 77-81)   Getting Organized (pages 263-267)

The

PROCESS of Writing

"The Process of Writing" section in *Write on Track* contains everything your students need to know about writing—from a basic look at the steps in the writing process to a discussion of writing with computers, from guidelines for writing paragraphs to guidelines for combining sentences. Once your students become familiar with all of this information they will turn to this section again and again, whenever they have a question about their writing. The table of contents below lists all of the chapters in "The Process of Writing" section of the handbook. The page numbers refer to the location of each chapter summary in this guide.

Special Note: For minilessons related to the writing process, see pages 101-109.

Getting Started

Prewriting and Drafting Guide

Revising, Conferencing, and Editing Guide

Building Paragraphs

Building Sentences

All About Writing

(pages 13-15)

In her book, *Living Between the Lines*, Lucy McCormick Calkins states, "The reason many of us care so much about the teaching of reading and writing is that when we give the children the words they need, we are giving them life and growth and refreshment." Her words provide a perfect introduction to the opening part of *Write on Track*. We believe that the information in "The Process of Writing" helps "give the words" students need to live and grow as young writers.

The first chapter, **All About Writing**, opens with a young writer's thoughts about writing. An analysis of her ideas illustrates three important points about writing—that it can be fun, that it is a way to "talk" to others, and that it is a way to learn. The steps in the writing process—from prewriting through publishing—are graphically presented on the next two pages. Read and discuss this brief chapter at the beginning of the year.

Rationale

- **Writing helps students learn about themselves and the world around them.**
- **Writing is a process of developing and exploring more than it is an end product.**
- **The writing process provides students with a basic framework, or blueprint, helping them learn and grow as writers.**

Major Concepts

* Writing is many different things, including a satisfying way to share and to learn. (page 13)
* The process of writing involves prewriting, drafting, revising, editing and proofreading, and publishing. (pages 14-15)

The Process of Writing **39**

One Writer's Process

(pages 16-19)

Most young writers, especially if they are new to the writing process, don't appreciate that writing must go through a series of changes before it becomes effective. Once they get all of their ideas on paper, they feel that their writing is essentially complete, except perhaps for making a few surface changes. As you know, and as your students must learn, one draft is not enough. (Boldly display those last five words in your classroom!) Real writing, writing that speaks clearly and completely, results from drafting *and* careful revising and editing.

One Writer's Process shows how one young writer developed a personal story using the steps in the writing process. Students see planning, drafting, revising, and editing in action. They see firsthand how making changes—from moving ideas to changing specific words—turns a first draft into an engaging piece of writing.

Rationale

● **Seeing the writing process in action helps students understand how it works.**

● **The writing process is a series of choices a writer makes as she or he develops an idea.**

Major Concepts

✱ Prewriting involves selecting a subject and collecting details. (page 16)

✱ A first draft is a first look at a developing writing idea. (page 17)

✱ Revising means making improvements in a piece of writing. (page 18)

✱ Editing and proofreading means checking for errors in usage, punctuation, grammar, and spelling. (page 18)

Writing with a Computer

(pages 20-25)

Students love computers. They're eager to use them at any time, for any purpose. (Students are generally enthused about *all* technology.) As educators, we must share in this enthusiasm and come to appreciate the computer as a valuable learning tool, especially when it comes to writing. To do otherwise, would be to ignore some very encouraging research about computer-assisted writing: Computers help students stay with a piece of writing longer. They make revising more accessible. They promote collaboration. They build self-esteem, and so on.

Writing with a Computer serves as an effective starting point for student writers who are ready to go on-line. The chapter contains a diagram of a personal computer as well as background information about using a computer and working with a keyboard. The charts on the last two pages will help students practice keyboarding.

Rationale

● **The personal computer is an important writing and learning tool.**

● **Computers address individual needs.**

● **Computers help students appreciate writing as a process.**

Major Concepts

✻ The computer is one of a writer's best friends. (page 20)

✻ It's important to know the basic parts of a personal computer. (page 21)

✻ It's important to understand how to use a computer as a writing tool. (page 22)

✻ Writing with a computer requires knowledge of the keyboard. (pages 23-25)

Planning Portfolios

(pages 26-29)

Planning Portfolios introduces students to two types of portfolios: the personal portfolio and the classroom portfolio. A *personal portfolio* is a place for students to collect their writing for their own use. A *classroom portfolio* is a place for students to showcase their best writing in school.

Personal portfolios help young writers keep track of all of their work—from stories to poems to secret writing. Classroom writing portfolios serve three important purposes: (1) They help teachers assess each student's development as a writer and learner. (2) They get students actively involved in the writing/learning process. (3) They allow parents to see firsthand how their child is progressing as a writer. (The last point assumes parents will be given the opportunity to review their child's portfolio.)

Rationale

● **Planning and compiling a portfolio provides students with an excellent opportunity to learn and to grow as a writer.**

● **Classroom portfolios provide an authentic means of assessment.**

● **Portfolios require students to reflect upon their writing.**

Major Concepts

* A portfolio is a special collection of an individual's writing. (page 26)

* A personal portfolio can be set up in different ways. (page 27)

* A classroom portfolio includes writing examples plus evaluation sheets. (page 28)

* Developing an effective classroom portfolio requires careful planning and organizing. (page 29)

Publishing Your Writing

(pages 30-33)

Publishing makes writing real. It gets young writers interested in their work, and it helps them take greater pride in it. It underscores the importance of planning, drafting, and revising. It provides an opportunity to receive praise and recognition. It nurtures an awareness of authorship and audience. Publishing is to writing what a live performance is to a musician. By taking center stage, a writer finds out how well he or she is doing, and how he or she might do even better the next time.

Publishing Your Writing begins with a basic definition of publishing as sharing a piece of writing. The chapter then suggests other ways students can publish their best writing. (Sharing a piece of writing with their writing group and teacher is the most immediate and, by far, the most helpful form of publishing for students.)

Rationale

- ● **Publishing is an integral part of the writing process.**
- ● **Seeing one's own work published builds self-esteem.**
- ● **Publishing promotes risk taking and closer attention to style, structure, and language.**

Major Concepts

- ✳ Publishing is the last step in the writing process. (page 30)
- ✳ There are many ways to publish writing, including sharing a final draft with classmates. (pages 30-33)

Building a File of Writing Ideas

(pages 35-37)

For most professionals, writing is a way of life that affects and directs almost all of their actions. In one sense, the pros never stop writing—no matter if they are walking to the mailbox, reading a magazine, or simply doodling on a napkin. They are constantly observing and absorbing ideas they can use in their stories and essays. Here's what two well-known authors have to say about the writer's life:

> *I'm always storing up images and expressions in my memory file that I can flip through and draw upon when I'm actually working.*
> —Steven Kellogg

> *I always scribble down ideas when I get them. I find that so many ideas come to me that if I don't write them down, they're gone.*
> —Jane Yolen

Building a File of Writing Ideas encourages students to think and act like writers by becoming more observant, by keeping track of important events, by reading a lot, and by writing regularly in a journal or notebook. The main point in this chapter is very simple: If students take the time to look, listen, and learn, they will discover plenty of interesting things to write about.

Rationale

- **Experienced writers are always collecting ideas for their work.**
- **Writing is more than putting words on paper. It is reading, observing, listening, and reflecting.**
- **Writing becomes rewarding when it stems from a writer's interests and concerns.**

Major Concepts

* It's important to keep track of good writing ideas in a notebook. (page 35)
* Students can build a file of writing ideas in many different ways. (pages 36-37)

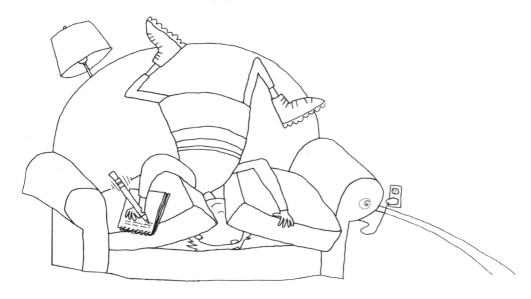

Collecting Details

(pages 38-39)

In *Investigate Nonfiction* (Heinemann 1989), Donald Graves says, "Children should write from an abundance of information." Information empowers students; it provides them with incentive to write because they have knowledge to share. Information gathering is especially important for students in grades 3-6 as they begin to write reports and essays. Thus, teachers in these grades have the important task of helping students become information gatherers.

Collecting Details touches on the three basic ways to acquire information: gathering facts from printed material and technology, talking to other people, and collecting your own thoughts. It also offers five ways for students to collect and clarify their own thoughts about a topic.

Rationale

- **Learning how to learn (how to acquire knowledge) should be an integral part of a writing program.**
- **Collecting details is an important aspect of prewriting.**
- **"Students must be given opportunities to assert their expertise over some body of knowledge." (Graves)**

Major Concepts

∗ Details are the facts and ideas that make writing interesting. (page 38)

∗ Collecting details includes researching, talking, and brainstorming. (pages 38-39)

∗ Listing, answering the 5 W's, and clustering are effective ways to collect ideas. (page 39)

Planning Notes

Chapter Links: The following chapters in the handbook also address collecting information:

* "Reading to Understand," pages 200-205
* "Getting Organized," pages 263-267

Planning and Drafting Guide

(pages 40-41)

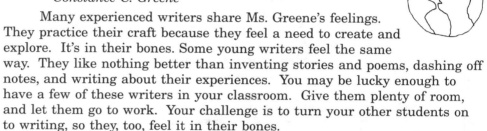

*" 'Are you still writing?'
people ask me in a slightly
jocular tone. . . . 'Are you
still breathing?' I could reply;
and do not. Once started,
it's tough to stop."*
—Constance C. Greene

Many experienced writers share Ms. Greene's feelings.
They practice their craft because they feel a need to create and
explore. It's in their bones. Some young writers feel the same
way. They like nothing better than inventing stories and poems, dashing off
notes, and writing about their experiences. You may be lucky enough to
have a few of these writers in your classroom. Give them plenty of room,
and let them go to work. Your challenge is to turn your other students on
to writing, so they, too, feel it in their bones.

Your job will be made a lot easier if you establish a writer-friendly
classroom based on the following principles:

1. Writing is a process more than it is an end product.
2. Young writers should write about subjects that interest them.
3. They should share their work throughout the writing process.
4. They should write with sincere and genuine feelings.
5. They should write for real readers.

These principles guided us as we developed all of the writing chapters
in *Write on Track*. The **Planning and Drafting Guide** chapter, for example, pays
special attention to points one and five. It addresses aspects of prewriting
and drafting, two steps in the writing process. And it gets young writers to
think about their work in terms of their readers and other key points like
purpose and form.

Rationale

- **Students will be more committed to writing if it is approached with a real plan and purpose in mind.**
- **The beginning of a piece of writing should grab the readers' attention.**
- **A first draft is a writer's first look at an emerging writing idea.**

Major Concepts

* Before students carry out a first draft, they should identify four key points about their writing. (page 40)

* It's important to pay special attention to the beginning part of a draft. (page 41)

* The purpose of a first draft is not to write a perfect paper, but to get all of the ideas on paper. (page 41)

Revising Your Writing

(pages 43-47)

Writers improve upon what they have written by rereading their work and rewriting the parts that need to be changed. This process is called *revision*. Among other things, writers read and listen for meaning, voice, authority, and design. Revision is important for all writers, not only because it provides an opportunity to make a draft better, but because it also frees the writer to take risks much earlier in the process.

Using the story of Pinocchio, **Revising Your Writing** begins by drawing an analogy between wood carving and revising. Suggestions for ways to get started come next, followed by ideas about what to look for in good writing. For example, we give advice about checking the three main parts in a piece of writing: the beginning, the middle, and the ending. This is followed by a discussion of using sensory detail in writing. The chapter ends with a revision checklist.

Rationale

- **Many students think that good writers sit down and write finished, polished pieces the first time through. This rarely happens.**

- **When young writers see that time away from their draft will help them find its strong and weak points, they will feel better about taking risks early on.**

- **Information about the revision process can lead to a healthy understanding about how good writing gets done.**

Major Concepts

* Writing can be changed to make it better. (page 43)

* Writers can revise alone or with friends. (page 44)

* When revising alone, it helps to read the draft out loud. (page 44)

* Beginnings need to interest readers and tell the subject. (page 45)

* The middle of a draft needs to stay on the topic. (page 45)

* Endings should remind readers about the subject and be interesting. (page 45)

* Writers can bring their writing to life by using the five senses. (page 46)

Conferencing with Partners

(pages 48-51)

When children talk about their writing to others, they are holding a conference. The process of conferring with partners gives writers insight, which in turn helps them gain control over their writing process.

Conferencing with Partners begins by reminding students that people with the same job or goal talk to one another in order to do their best work. The handbook suggests that through conferring, like-minded individuals discover strengths, get new ideas, fix problems, and find mistakes. Writer and listener guidelines are laid out next, to show students how to make the most of their conferencing time. Then the handbook lists conferencing suggestions for each part of the writing process. The chapter ends with two types of response sheets, which encourage students to write comments about their peers' writing.

Rationale

● **As writers review their own writing, they try to look at it with "new eyes." It follows that another approach is to literally bring in others' eyes.**

● **Almost any friendly response helps sustain children's interest in their writing.**

● **When conferring is part of a writing program, students learn how to talk about writing and how to receive and use information from others.**

Major Concepts

✱ Students with similar goals can help one another do their best work. (page 48)

✱ When conferring, certain actions promote success. (page 49)

✱ Students can confer throughout the writing process. (page 50)

✱ Writing down responses is a good way to help students gather their thoughts for a fruitful conference. (page 51)

Editing  and Proofreading

(pages 52-53)

Editing and Proofreading offers specific guidelines for preparing writing for publication. It is stated in the introductory paragraph that this step becomes important *after* the main ideas in the writing have been improved, or revised. The checklist on the second page covers sentence clarity, word choice, punctuation, spelling, and capitalization.

The chapter points out that it is difficult for writers to edit and proofread without help. Publishing companies employ editors and proofreaders to help professional writers make their writing as clear and correct as it can be. Students must do this job for each other (or with the help of a teacher or parent) by checking their partner's work for clarity and for surface errors.

Rationale

- **Work put on public display needs to be correct.**
- **Errors make it difficult for readers to appreciate a piece of writing.**
- **Editing and proofreading each other's work helps develop a community of student writers.**

Major Concepts

* Editing and proofreading gets writing ready to be shared. (page 52)

* Editing and proofreading is a shared process. (page 52)

* A sentence check is an important part of editing. (page 53)

* Choosing interesting as well as correct words is an important editing job. (page 53)

* Punctuation, spelling, and capitalization are also important parts of editing and proofreading. (page 53)

Planning Notes

Speaking Connections: Hold periodic editor's chair meetings, where editors share interesting words and well-constructed long sentences (or ways they've found to combine short sentences) in their editing.

Writing Paragraphs

(pages 54-63)

A stand-alone paragraph presents a story, a description, an opinion, or an explanation about a specific subject. The type of paragraph that is written depends upon the subject and the purpose of the writing. No matter what form a paragraph takes, it must contain enough supporting details to give the reader a clear and interesting picture of the subject.

Writing Paragraphs begins with a definition of a paragraph *(several sentences, all about the same subject)*. The basic parts of a paragraph are discussed next. Then examples of the four basic types of paragraphs (narrative, descriptive, expository, and persuasive) are provided. The chapter ends with a detailed explanation of how to write a paragraph.

Rationale

- **Real-world writing (news articles, directions to a specific place, requests, simple explanations of how to do something) often involves the construction of simple paragraphs.**

- **Paragraphs are the conceptual building blocks for stories, essays, and articles. Writing them gives children the opportunity to think conceptually.**

- **Understanding the idea of "paragraph" helps children edit their work: they will be better able to find where their drafts need paragraph breaks.**

Major Concepts

* A paragraph is a group of sentences that tells about one specific subject or idea. (page 55)

* Paragraphs have three basic parts: the topic sentence, the body, and the closing sentence. (pages 56-57)

* There are four types of paragraphs, each with its own function. (pages 58-61)

* Information presented in a paragraph needs to be ordered. (page 62)

* Revising a paragraph involves checking for clarity and coherence. (page 63)

Writing a Summary

(pages 64-67)

Summary writing helps students develop competence as critical thinkers, pulling together important reading and writing skills. As the handbook metaphor of "panning for gold" points out (page 64), when your students write summaries, they are learning how to find the main ideas in reading material. Learning how to express these ideas succinctly in their own words is the other side of the gold coin.

Writing a Summary begins by explaining the definition and purpose of a summary. A model summary is given, along with the text from which it was derived. Then students are guided through a step-by-step process to write their own summaries.

Rationale

- ● **Summarizing helps students process information.**
- ● **Writing summaries helps students think more critically.**
- ● **Summary writing plays an important role in many areas of the curriculum.**

Major Concepts

- * Summarizing is a useful writing and learning skill. (page 64)
- * A summary writer must be a careful reader. (page 66)
- * You need to write a summary in your own words. (page 67)
- * The first sentence of a summary is very important. (page 67)

Planning Notes

Across-the-Curriculum Possibilities: It is valuable for students to make frequent oral and/or written summaries of material they are studying. After students read a science chapter, for example, ask for summaries.

School and Community Uses: Ask students to summarize special events: assemblies, field trips, class performances, and so on. A monthly "School Summary Sheet" can be sent home, thus using students' developing skills to build community ties.

Writing Basic Sentences

(pages 69-71)

The sentence is a building block of communication. We write sentences; we speak sentences; and we read them. Helping students develop their sentence sense must be a primary objective in any language-arts curriculum. This objective can best be met by immersing students in the language. If they are engaged in all sorts of writing, reading, speaking, and listening activities, their sentence sense will develop naturally and effectively. To what extent you get into the technical aspects of sentences (naming the parts of a sentence, identifying the different types, etc.) depends upon the needs of your students and the demands of your curriculum.

Writing Basic Sentences discusses sentence parts (subject and verb) and sentence problems (fragments, run-on sentences, and rambling sentences). When you are ready to introduce your students to basic sentence structure and sentence correctness, this chapter serves as the perfect starting point.

Rationale

● **Students must develop their sentence sense in order to express themselves effectively.**

● **Students need a basic understanding of the "grammar" of sentences.**

Major Concepts

✱ We use sentences all the time in our writing, reading, and speaking. (page 69)

✱ A sentence is not complete unless it has a subject and a verb. (page 70)

✱ Fragments, run-ons, and rambling sentences are three common sentence errors. (page 71)

Planning Notes

Chapter Links: The following chapters in the handbook explore sentence structure and sentence style:
* "Combining Sentences," pages 72-73
* "Understanding Sentences," pages 324-327

Combining Sentences

(pages 72-73)

Writing clear and accurate sentences is challenge enough for most young writers. When they edit their work, they ask practical questions like these: *Do my sentences make sense? Did I start each one with a capital letter?* Concern about the sound and flow of the writing is a bit beyond most of them. But that's okay. Their sense of sentence style will develop naturally as they write more and more. You'll be doing your students a great service, stylistically speaking, if you simply encourage them to . . .

> * experiment with many forms of writing,
> * write about subjects that are important to them,
> * and "speak" in words that sound genuine and real.

You can also introduce them to sentence combining (but do so later in the year). Basically speaking, sentence combining helps young writers turn short, choppy ideas into longer sentences that read more smoothly.

The **Combining Sentences** chapter in *Write on Track* begins with an example to show students how combining ideas can make writing more interesting and easier to read. Then four combining techniques are discussed: combining with a series, with key words, with compound subjects, and with compound verbs.

Rationale

● **Stylistic writing is characterized by various combinations of long and short sentences.**

● **Sentence combining helps students see the variety of word combinations available to them.**

● **Sentence combining enhances students' editing skills.**

Major Concepts

* Sentence combining is making one longer sentence out of two or more shorter sentences. (page 72)

* Short sentences can be combined in many ways. (page 73)

Planning Notes

Chapter Link: The following handbook chapter will help you implement "Combining Sentences":
   * "Understanding Sentences," pages 324-327

The **FORMS** of Writing

You can build a timely and comprehensive writing program around "The Forms of Writing" section in *Write on Track*. Included in this section of the handbook are guidelines for writing personal narratives, book reviews, business letters, poems, plays, and much more. The table of contents below lists all the chapters in "The Forms of Writing" section of the handbook. The page numbers refer to the location of each chapter summary in this guide.

Special Note: For minilessons related to the forms of writing, see pages 110-119.

Personal Writing

Subject Writing

Research Writing

Writing Stories, Tales, and Plays

Writing Poems

Writing in Journals

(pages 77-81)

A journal can be a notebook with blank pages or a simple, stapled stack of paper. Journals demonstrate to students that their observations, interests, and ideas count and can become important notes for more extended writing.

Writing in Journals begins by telling students there are three kinds of journals: a personal journal, a reading journal, and a learning log. Suggestions for personal journal writing include the following: recording interesting sights and sounds, collecting ideas for stories and poems, preserving memories of happy (and not so happy) times, collecting and writing secret letters and notes. The reading journal section provides example entries for an autobiography, a riddle book, and a nonfiction book. Writing in a learning log shows how students use journal writing to explain their thinking in mathematics, to practice close observation of an object, and to ask questions about a topic in social studies. Finally, students see how pictures or diagrams can be useful in a learning log.

Rationale

● **Students learn by writing.**

● **Fluency grows from writing regularly in journals. This fluency extends to other types of writing.**

● **Journal writing becomes the source for more extended writing.**

Major Concepts

✱ Students can keep journals—just the way their favorite authors do. (page 77)

✱ Students keep personal journals on a variety of topics. (page 78)

✱ Reading journals are places to write about books students read. (page 79)

✱ Learning logs are a special kind of journal for writing about subjects across the curriculum. (page 80)

Making Albums

(pages 82-83)

An album is a child's keepsake book, a place to keep memories. It is a place, or a way, for children to organize a special part of their lives. Collecting items in an album gives children a sense of control. It satisfies something very basic—the need to gather, arrange, and preserve.

Making Albums begins by explaining that an album may be a place to collect things such as stamps or coins or baseball cards. The point is made that the greatest qualification for making an album is to be interested in something. Guidelines for making a pet or best-friend album are provided.

Rationale

● **Setting up and adding to an album gives students a fun way to practice keeping track of things, a precursor to study skills.**

● **Through collecting and arranging objects they care about in albums, students develop organizational abilities.**

● **There is special appeal—and value—in writing factual documentation about something you care about.**

Major Concepts

✱ There are many kinds of albums. (page 82)

✱ The handbook guides students through a three-step process to create an album about a pet or a friend. (page 83)

Planning Notes

Materials Needed: An album can be made from a notebook or a stack of paper stapled together. Students can design special covers from construction paper, wallpaper samples, or file folders.

Reading/Writing Connections: *My Book about My Dog* and *My Book about My Cat*, both by Sheldon Gerstenfeld, V.M.D., (Bantam 1994) are fun-filled keepsake albums, inviting children to fill in the appropriate information.

My Pet: A PhotoLog Book by Janet Horowitz and Kathy Faggella (Stewart, Tabori & Chang 1992) treats the young writer like an investigative reporter uncovering information about a pet.

School and Community Uses: When the albums are completed students can share their work with other classes. The finished products can be put on display.

Writing Lists

(pages 84-87)

"Listing is a remarkable generator for any writer. We [list] all the time, but it doesn't occur to us that we're actually using our lists to think." So says Peter Stillman in his book *Families Writing* (Writer's Digest Books 1989). We agree that list making is a "remarkable" writing technique, especially for young writers. List making opens up a writer's mind, it unlocks a writer's best ideas, and it proves to any writer, young or old, that they have plenty to write about.

Writing Lists begins with a list to get things done—a shopping list. Then students are introduced to imaginary lists, lists of happy things, and lists of crazy things (a literary connection). Models are provided to inspire students to write their own lists.

Rationale

- **Lists help students generate ideas.**
- **Lists help students organize their ideas.**
- **Lists promote logical and creative thinking.**

Major Concepts

* Lists can serve many purposes. (page 84)

* Lists can help us express our feelings. (pages 85-86)

* Lists can expand our world, helping us to see new relationships. (page 86)

* Lists can become an organizing principle for writing. (page 87)

Planning Notes

Reading/Writing Connections: Your library is a good resource for lists. For starters, many children find Shel Silverstein's "Sarah Cynthia Sylvia Stout Would Not Take the Garbage Out" irresistible (in *Where the Sidewalk Ends,* Harper and Row 1974). They will ask for this list poem again and again.

The prize-winning *One Gorilla* by Atsuko Morozumi (Farrar Straus Giroux 1990) contains a list of the things the narrator loves, and it gets students thinking about what they like a lot.

Across-the-Curriculum Possibilities: You can use list making in science and social studies as a useful study skill. Ask children to list the major points in the chapter they have read.

Writing Friendly Notes

(pages 88-91)

Writing Friendly Notes emphasizes the directness of writing quick notes to friends and acquaintances. Notes are characterized as even more user-friendly than the traditional friendly letter.

This chapter begins by explaining how friendly notes are very quick and easy to write. The following reasons for writing notes are discussed: to say thank you, to ask for a favor, to send a special message, and to share something you know. The chapter concludes with ideas for adding special touches to friendly notes.

Rationale

● **Writing friendly notes gives children the opportunity to write spontaneously about topics they care about.**

● **Friendly notes provide immediate reinforcement from the recipients.**

● **Writing can be a way to cement friendships.**

Major Concepts

* Friendly notes are fun for the writer and the recipient. (page 88)

* Friendly notes are short and varied in format. (page 88)

* People write friendly notes for a variety of reasons. (pages 89-91)

Planning Notes

Materials Needed: You may want to have a supply of appealing stationery, construction paper, colored pencils, pens, rubber stamps, and stickers for your students to use.

Reading/Writing Connections: *How to Make Pop-Ups* by Joan Irvine (1988) provides directions for creating fantastic pop-up cards. Students can turn their creations into super friendly notes. The bonus is that students gain practice in reading carefully and following directions when they make their creations.

School and Community Uses: There are many people right in the school community—the principal and assistant principal, the cooks, the crossing guard, the janitor, and so on—who would love to receive friendly notes from students.

Writing Friendly **Letters**

(pages 92-95)

The friendly letter is a natural form of writing for students. Like all of us, children like to get personal mail, and they learn quickly that the best way to get a letter is to send one.

Writing Friendly Letters begins with an introduction to and a description of the parts of a friendly letter. Then a student model is presented, followed by steps and guidelines for writing friendly letters.

Rationale

● **Writing a friendly letter gives children the opportunity to write about topics they care about.**

● **Receiving letters encourages students to write more.**

● **Learning how to communicate in writing is an important social skill.**

● **Letter writing promotes fluency in all writing.**

Major Concepts

✳ A friendly letter has a heading, salutation, body, closing, and signature. (pages 92-93)

✳ Good letters result from planning and revising. (pages 94-95)

Planning Notes

Materials Needed: You may want to have a supply of appealing stationery, colored pencils, pens, rubber stamps, ink pads, and stickers for your students to use.

Reading/Writing Connections: *Mouse Letters* (E. P. Dutton 1993) by Michelle Cartlidge is a tiny book containing tiny letters written by mouse fairies and left in real envelopes for readers to enjoy. These winsome letters are sure to inspire students to create their own letter books.

Yours Affectionately, Peter Rabbit (Viking Press 1984) by Beatrix Potter contains letters written by some of Potter's most popular characters. Encourage students to think of other literary characters who might enjoy writing to each other.

Across-the-Curriculum Possibilities: *Your Best Friend Kate* (Macmillan 1989) and *Kate Heads West* (Macmillan 1990) by Pat Brisson provide charming models of friendly letters—to friends, family members, teachers, and even a dentist. As Kate travels around the country, documenting vacation fun, she also gives readers an informal lesson in geography.

Writing Personal Narratives

(pages 96-99)

Many experienced writers say that all writing begins with narrative. And the first stories, the most basic ones, come from an individual's own life. That is why it is so important, and so natural, to have your students write personal narratives throughout the school year. At first, your students will (or should) be concerned with getting all of their facts and details straight. Then, as they become more experienced, they may show more concern about their feelings related to their personal stories. Watch for this development in the narratives they write.

Writing Personal Narratives begins with a short discussion of how most narratives begin—as real-life stories we tell our friends. This short introduction leads into a student model and suggestions for listing and selecting possible topics. Guidelines for writing, revising, editing, and proofreading follow.

Rationale

● **Writing personal narratives helps children establish an identity and gain self-confidence.**

● **When we hear others' personal narratives, it helps us see our similarities and understand our differences.**

Major Concepts

✳ A personal narrative is a story about a personal memory. (page 96)

✳ Students can use the writing process to write a good personal story. (pages 98-99)

✳ Students can enrich their stories with details and dialogue. (page 99)

Planning Notes

Materials Needed: It would be helpful to have many personal narratives in the classroom. Go beyond books and find personal narratives in magazines such as *Cricket, Stone Soup, Skipping Stones: A Multicultural Children's Quarterly*, and *The Daybreak Star Indian Reader.*

Reading/Writing Connections: As you read and discuss personal narratives in the classroom, pay special attention to the choice of topics (noting that topics are sometimes everyday events), the use of dialogue, and the inclusion of specific details.

School and Community Uses: The magazines listed above (except *Cricket*) all publish children's personal narratives. Also, younger children benefit from hearing what life is like in the upper grades. Let your students share their personal narratives with younger students.

Writing Family Stories

(pages 100-103)

Family stories show us how families are unique, and how much they have in common. Families tell stories over and over to inspire, to amuse, and to entertain. These are the stories that identify a family. Students should become aware that in working hard to craft a family story they are giving their families a precious gift.

Writing Family Stories provides two models that are sure to entertain and inspire students to write their own stories. The guidelines in the chapter help students at each step in the writing process, from choosing a subject to sharing a first draft to checking the revised writing for errors.

Rationale

● **Family stories encourage students to write within an existing story structure.**

● **Retelling a story helps young writers learn to organize information and sequence events.**

Major Concepts

* Family stories express every emotion. (page 100)

* Family stories can come from a writer's own experience or from a story told by a relative. (page 101)

* Students can learn to write a family story using the writing process. (pages 102-103)

Planning Notes

Speaking Connections: Hearing a teacher tell a family story inspires students to tell their own stories. Also encourage students to tell a story to a buddy or small group before trying to write it.

Reading/Writing Connections: Many authors favored by third graders write family stories. Picture book are especially helpful as writing models, focusing as they do on one incident. Donald Crew's *Shortcut* (Greenwillow 1992) is a great family story, focusing on one dramatic incident from this popular author-illustrator's own childhood. For teachers, *Families Writing* by Peter Stillman (Writer's Digest Books 1989) is a wonderful, wise, and practical resource of writing ideas.

Across-the-Curriculum Possibilities: In this era of mobility, children hear lots of stories about the places where their grandparents and great-grandparents were born. These birthplace stories offer opportunitues for map study and research.

School and Community Uses: Family stories provide good material for dramatization. ("Writing Plays," pages 170-175 in the handbook, will help students turn their stories into scripts.)

Writing Alphabet Books

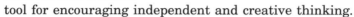

(pages 105-109)

Poet Norma Farber calls alphabet books her love letters to children. Teachers who introduce such love letters into their curriculums quickly discover a marvelous tool for encouraging independent and creative thinking.

Writing Alphabet Books begins with a popular jump-rope jingle, "My name is Alice and my husband's name is Al," an invitation for students to have fun with language. Student models follow, illustrating another type of alphabet format: the information organizer. A four-step process guides students as they create their own alphabet books. The chapter ends with another model and suggestions for getting started on a zany alphabet creation.

Rationale

- The ABC format encourages students to have fun with language.
- The ABC format helps students learn to organize information.
- The ABC format provides a way for students to learn sentence structure.

Major Concepts

* Nearly any topic can be organized and understood by its alphabetic components. (page 105)

* Writing alphabet books is fun as well as challenging. (page 106)

* Students can learn to write an alphabet book using a four-step process. (pages 107-108)

Planning Notes

Materials Needed: Reading alphabet books is the best way to encourage students to write them. Have a broad collection in your classroom. Also have bookmaking materials: various sizes of paper and cardboard as well as a variety of colored pencils, pens, and markers.

Reading/Writing Connections: *The Little Cats ABC Book* by Martin Leman (Simon & Schuster 1993) lists cats' names from A to Z and is sure to inspire dog lovers to try writing one for their favorite pet. *Alphabestiary*, edited by Jane Yolen (Boyds Mills Press 1995), offers poems about animals from A to Z.

Chapter Link: The following chapter in the handbook will help students make and bind their alphabet books:
    * "Publishing Your Writing," pages 30-33

Writing Newspaper Stories

(pages 110-115)

Third grade is often a time when students are eager to reach out to the world in their writing. A class newspaper provides the perfect format to inspire these young writers.

Writing Newspaper Stories begins by distinguishing between two kinds of stories in a student newspaper, the news story and the human interest story. A third part of the student paper, letters to the editor, is also described.

A model news story is provided and the parts delineated. Students are then taken through the process of writing a news story, including using the 5 W's. A model human interest story and letter to the editor are also given, with important points emphasized in marginal notes.

Rationale

● **The real-world nature of newspaper writing gives it importance and allure.**

● **Newspaper writing emphasizes many qualities of good writing—clarity, coherence, accuracy, and so on.**

Major Concepts

✱ A news story has a specific structure. (pages 111, 113)

✱ A newswriter has the responsibility to collect information. (page 112)

✱ News and human interest stories need strong leads. (pages 111, 113-114)

✱ Writing a letter to the editor is one of the most important ways to practice freedom of expression and freedom of the press. (page 115)

Planning Notes

Materials Needed: Students enjoy having special reporter tools. These can be notebooks or clipboards. If students are interviewing someone, they may want to use a tape recorder, though they are likely to find transcribing difficult.

Reading/Writing Connections: Have at least one local newspaper in the classroom each day. Find items you can read to the class.

Chapter Links: The following chapters in the handbook will help students with their work in "Writing Newspaper Stories":
* "Writing Business Letters," pages 122-129
* "Learning to Interview," pages 252-255

Writing Book **Reviews**

(pages 116-121)

A book review answers questions that readers often wonder about before they decide to read a book. Most students like to know which books their friends are reading and what the books are about. Students will enjoy writing and reading book reviews if the right tone is set in the classroom.

Writing Book Reviews opens with a short discussion on sharing feelings about books. The following pages contain two book reviews by students, clear and simple writing guidelines, and a helpful collection chart. The chapter ends with a list of words often used in reviews.

Rationale

● **Book reviews give students opportunities to write about books they care about.**

● **Book reviews give students opportunities to write persuasively.**

● **Writing book reviews brings reading and writing skills together and demonstrates comprehension.**

Major Concepts

✱ A book review provides an opportunity to share feelings. (page 116)

✱ A basic book review answers three questions: (1) What is the book about? (2) Why do I like the book? (3) What message did the author share? (page 119)

✱ Reviewers use a special vocabulary when they talk about books. (page 121)

Planning Notes

Materials Needed: Books with jackets or writing on the back covers often provide models for answering the basic book-review questions, so have some books of this type available. Models of student book reviews would also be helpful.

Reading/Writing Connections: Encourage students to write freely in their reading journals about the books they read. (See page 79 in the handbook for information about reading journals.) Journal entries will help students write book reviews.

Across-the-Curriculum Possibilities: Writing book reviews across the curriculum promotes the reading of nonfiction books. Students will have a chance to discover how interesting subject reading can be.

School and Community Uses: Doctors' waiting rooms are useful places for your classroom's book-review collections. Book stores frequently post student-written reviews as well. Short reviews can also be a regular part of school announcements.

Writing Business Letters

(pages 122-129)

The business letter may be a new form for many of your students, bringing a real-life context to the classroom. Students will have the opportunity to request information or suggest a solution to a problem, and have the excitement of getting mail back.

Writing Business Letters begins by explaining the difference between a friendly letter and a business letter. Two types of business letters are then discussed. The chapter explains the six parts of a business letter and identifies each part in a student model letter. Guidelines for writing a business letter are provided, as is information about folding a letter and addressing an envelope.

Rationale

● **The business letter is a real-world writing form that students can use to get action and recognition.**

● **Students usually receive serious responses when they write well-planned letters. This demonstrates the power of the written word.**

● **The ability to write a clear business letter is a lifelong benefit.**

Major Concepts

✳ The two types of business letters introduced are a letter asking for information and a letter suggesting how to solve a problem. (pages 125, 128)

✳ All types of business letters have a common format: heading, inside address, salutation, body, closing, and signature. (pages 124-125)

✳ Writing a business letter is a step-by-step process. (pages 126-127)

✳ There is an accepted way to fold and address a business letter. (page 129)

Planning Notes

Materials Needed: You will need some business envelopes and stamps for this unit.

Reading/Writing Connections: In *Yours Affectionately, Peter Rabbit* by Beatrix Potter there is an exchange of letters among the characters. Squirrel Nutkin, for example, writes several business letters to Mr. Brown, asking for his tail back. (Invite your students to compose business letters on behalf of favorite literary characters.)

Across-the-Curriculum Possibilities: Once they've learned the form, students can assume some of the classroom business correspondence: book-club problems, information needed for a science project, and so on.

Writing to Explain

(pages 130-135)

Writing explanations will be a new experience for many third graders. But it is a form they will find increasingly useful (and important) as they advance in school. In a social studies class, they may be asked to explain how a certain part of government works, in science they may be asked to explain a process, and so on.

Writing to Explain, in the opening paragraph, makes an important point about this form—that some explanations help us *understand* things, and others help us *do* things. Also included on the introductory page is a fun set of directions for students to try. Complete guidelines for writing directions follow. The rest of the chapter contains a wonderful collection of model explanations.

Rationale

- Writing explanations helps students organize their thoughts.
- Writing explanations helps students sequence ideas and write clearly and precisely.
- Writing explanations has practical applications for students (giving directions, explaining experiments, and so on).

Major Concepts

* Explanations begin with a topic sentence (or a descriptive title), followed by clear, step-by-step directions. (pages 130-135)

* Action words (*put, stand, take*) tell the reader what to do. (pages 131, 133)

* Order words (*next, then, after*) help the reader follow each step. (page 131)

Planning Notes

Materials Needed: Have a number of cookbooks for children on hand. Science and invention books describing various processes and how things work would also provide useful models.

Reading/Writing Connections: After reviewing the model explanations in the handbook, challenge students to find their own sample explanations in books and magazines. We recommend two books: *Bees Dance and Whales Sing* by Margery Facklam for its explanations of animal communication and *Creepy Cuisine* by Lucy Monroe for its precise recipe directions.

Across-the-Curriculum Possibilities: Writing explanations can obviously play an important role throughout the school curriculum. The introduction on this page suggests a few cross-curricular applications. You and your colleagues will think of many more.

Using the Library

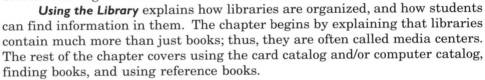

(pages 137-143)

The library may seem mysterious and overwhelming to some third-grade students. But once they learn some basic library skills, they'll be ready to take advantage of everything the library has to offer. When it comes to students and libraries, familiarity breeds learning and fun.

Using the Library explains how libraries are organized, and how students can find information in them. The chapter begins by explaining that libraries contain much more than just books; thus, they are often called media centers. The rest of the chapter covers using the card catalog and/or computer catalog, finding books, and using reference books.

Rationale

- Libraries are information storehouses that students need to learn about.
- Learning about the library helps students become researchers.
- Once students understand how the library works, they can use it more effectively.

Major Concepts

* Libraries contain not just books but also many other media. (page 137)

* Knowing how to use the card catalog and/or computer catalog helps students identify sources of information. (pages 138-140)

* Understanding how books are shelved helps students find the specific books they need. (page 141)

* Encyclopedias and other reference books contain information on a wide variety of subjects. (page 142)

* Understanding the parts of books helps students use them more effectively. (page 143)

Planning Notes

Materials Needed: Make arrangements with your school librarian (media specialist) so your students are in the library when you work with this chapter. Otherwise, bring to class the library resources covered in the chapter.

Writing Classroom Reports

(pages 144-151)

Third grade is a time for children to spread their wings, to begin making independent explorations. **Writing Classroom Reports** helps students use their own curiosity as a valuable research tool. They see that a good classroom report begins with what the writer likes and cares about. This chapter starts with a student's interest in hawks and then takes young writer-researchers through the steps in writing their own classroom report. A model report is included.

A great deal of attention is given to prewriting in this chapter. Selecting a subject, writing questions, researching the subject, organizing information—all of these important prewriting issues are addressed.

Rationale

● **Report writing is a way to tap into students' natural curiosity.**

● **Report writing helps students understand how nonfiction can be organized.**

● **Learning a method for keeping track of information is a valuable skill throughout school and throughout life.**

Major Concepts

* Choosing a topic you care about is important. (pages 144-145)

* Asking good questions is key to report writing. (pages 146, 147, 149)

* A gathering grid helps organize information. (page 148)

* A writer can use different strategies to hook readers' interest. (page 149)

Planning Notes

Reading/Writing/Listening Connections: Choose a nonfiction book to read aloud to the class—a book about a planet, for example. Before reading, ask students what questions they think the author might have asked about this topic. Write the questions on the board—and ask students to listen carefully to see if they are answered.

Across-the-Curriculum Possibilities: Invite questions from other classes on specified subjects: the solar system, the body, the U.S. Mint, etc. Students can research the questions and submit brief reports to the classes.

Teacher Resources: Here are two titles containing many report-writing ideas: *Doing What Scientists Do: Children Learn to Investigate Their World* by Ellen Doris (Heinemann 1991); *Discover: Investigate the Mysteries of History with 40 Practical Projects Probing Our Past* by Katherine Grier (Royal Ontario Museum/Addison-Wesley 1990).

Writing Photo Essays

(pages 152-157)

Myra Zarnowski says photo essays are the "show-and-tell" of writing. Using photos and words, writers show us and tell us about people, places, animals, and more.

Writing Photo Essays begins by acknowledging that books with photos are fun to read. The handbook mentions one particular photo essay as it explains the show-and-tell idea. Next comes a student model followed by planning, writing, and revising tips.

Rationale

● **Most children enjoy photo essays.**

● **Children's thinking skills are tapped as they learn how photos and text work together.**

● **Photo essays require research and decision making.**

● **The photo essay requires taking a point of view, which is a skill that should be nurtured throughout schooling.**

Major Concepts

✳ Photo essays are the show-and-tell of writing. (pages 152, 154)

✳ The photo essay needs to have a beginning, a middle, and an end. (pages 153-155)

✳ A photo essay will require research. (page 156)

✳ Words and pictures need to match. (page 157)

Planning Notes

Materials Needed: Have available cameras and film as well as materials to make books or posters.

Reading/Writing Connections: Maurice Sendak once said that he looks for "the crack in the text" when he draws pictures for books. What he meant is that he looks for information to put in his pictures that hasn't already been said in words (witness, for example, the pictures in *Where the Wild Things Are*). As you share photo essays with your class, talk about the idea of "the crack in the text" by asking children to tell what they see in the book's photos (or pictures) that isn't in the text, and discuss how the photos (or pictures) help understanding.

School and Community Uses: Writing a photo essay requires thoughtful decision making (e.g., what to write about, which pictures to take, which pictures to use, what words to use with each picture, what to ask at an interview, how to display the essay, and so on). Children who have been through this process could go on a "lecture tour," explaining to other groups of children how they went about making all these decisions.

Writing Realistic Stories

(pages 159-163)

A realistic story is based on something that really happened or could happen. In the past several decades *realistic fiction* has changed more than any other kind of literature for children (Sutherland and Arbuthnot 1991). We have more books by and about African-Americans, Asian-Americans, Native Americans, and Spanish-speaking people. Strong, popular interest in the elderly, the disabled, and many other social issues has also contributed to the revolution in this genre.

Writing Realistic Stories begins by explaining how realistic stories are different from fantasy stories and personal narratives. On the remaining pages, students will find a model, a writing approach, and some specific ideas for making realistic stories come to life.

Rationale

● **Writing realistic stories helps students appreciate that ideas for writing can come from their own lives.**

● **Writing through a make-believe character's point of view or about a slightly altered problem gives children the distance to reflect upon their own life and times.**

Major Concepts

✳ Realistic stories are always possible. (page 159)

✳ It's important to have a problem that needs to be solved. (page 161)

✳ First drafts can begin with real characters, problems, settings, and then be changed into fictional stories. (page 162)

✳ Action, dialogue, details, and word pictures help stories come alive for readers. (page 163)

Planning Notes

Reading/Writing Connection: Show children how the same topic can be handled differently by different authors. Comparing the books *High in the Mountain* by Ruth Radin (Orchard Books 1990) and *When I Was Young in the Mountains* by Cynthia Rylant (Dutton 1982) would demonstrate this well.

Across-the-Curriculum Possibilities: Animal reports can take the form of realistic fiction. See *Seasons of the Crane* by Peter Roop and Connie Roop (Walker & Co. 1989).

School and Community Uses: Children who come from other countries benefit from hearing the realistic stories written by their classmates. If possible, have people in your community translate these stories into the language of the emergent English speakers. Likewise, stories told in other languages could be translated into English.

Writing Time-Travel Fantasies

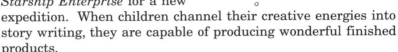

(pages 164-169)

Children invent imaginative scenarios all of the time when they play. On one day, they may be defending a castle, and on the next day, they may be preparing the *Starship Enterprise* for a new expedition. When children channel their creative energies into story writing, they are capable of producing wonderful finished products.

Writing Time-Travel Fantasies gives students an opportunity to use all of their creative writing skills. The chapter begins with "what if" questions presenting children with a few imaginative scenarios. Then they are asked to choose a time as the starting point for their own fantasy stories. The middle part of the chapter helps them develop their stories. The final two pages provide a model fantasy.

Rationale

● **When writing time-travel fantasies, third graders have a chance to learn about other times and places.**

● **Fantasy writing fosters three important creative thinking skills— flexibility, originality, and elaboration.**

Major Concepts

✳ Writing a fantasy often begins with writers asking "what if" questions. (page 164)

✳ When a story is placed in another time, it's important to learn about that time in order to create a believable setting. (page 165)

✳ The characters in a time-travel fantasy need a way to get to their new destination. (page 165)

✳ In addition to a setting, a time-travel fantasy needs characters who have a problem to solve. (page 166)

Planning Notes

Materials Needed: Have a collection of science fiction stories available for the students.

Reading/Writing Connection: As you share time-travel fantasies aloud, discuss how the main characters travel from one time period to another. For example, a train is used in *Time Train* by P. Fleischman, and a medallion is used in *Medallion of the Black Hound* by S. R. Murphy.

School and Community Uses: Have students develop simple games using their fantasy as a starting point. Send these games to other classes with the fantasies attached.

Writing Plays

(pages 170-175)

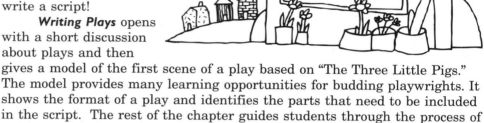

Writing a play can be an inviting experience for children, especially if the play is based on a familiar fairy tale or fable. Children of this age often create impromptu plays in school and in their free time. Now they will have the chance to preserve their plays by learning how to write a script!

Writing Plays opens with a short discussion about plays and then gives a model of the first scene of a play based on "The Three Little Pigs." The model provides many learning opportunities for budding playwrights. It shows the format of a play and identifies the parts that need to be included in the script. The rest of the chapter guides students through the process of writing a play for a fairy tale or fable.

Rationale

- **Writing plays allows students to apply their speaking skills to the written word.**

- **Plays are made up of dialogue—a form of language that third graders know as "the way people talk."**

- **Writing and performing plays demonstrate to students that their writing has an intended audience.**

Major Concepts

* Plays, like stories, have settings, characters, and problems to be solved. (page 170)

* A play is a kind of story that is acted out and told by characters (actors) who memorize a script. (page 175)

* Playwrights follow a special format when they write. (page 171)

Planning Notes

Materials Needed: In this chapter we ask children to choose a favorite tale or fable to adapt to play form. Provide plenty of picture books and anthologies of fairy tales and fables for the students.

Writing/Speaking Connections: Improvisation helps children understand and connect characters with dialogue. Involve children in acting out short scenes from stories. For example, have three children take the roles of the three bears talking while they wait for supper. Relate this procedure to creating dialogue for a play.

School and Community Uses: Students can perform their plays for other classes, for home-school meetings, or for nursing homes. If the "troupe" cannot take a play on the road, videotape a performance.

Writing Free-Verse Poetry

(pages 177-183)

Seeing, hearing, and feeling the language of poetry is what **Writing Free-Verse Poetry** is all about. Poets tell us why. Remembering the first poem she ever heard, Georgia Heard states, "It was about silver scales of fish and the ripples of water in a pond. I was astonished at what it made me see." Dylan Thomas said, "I had come to love just the words of them [poems], the words alone . . . the *sound*." When thinking about poetry, Myra Cohen Livingston talks of seeing oneself in a poem—feeling the language of poetry.

Writing Free-Verse Poetry begins with an idea: "Poetry is . . . what poetry does." It sings and dances. It laughs and cries. Students are shown how to make friends with a poem as they learn what makes poems special. They then try their hands at writing free-verse poetry, prewriting through proofreading. The chapter ends with a list of poetic techniques.

Rationale

- **Writing poetry offers students a personal and creative avenue for exploring and expressing their ideas, feelings, and imaginings.**
- **Writing poetry gives students an opportunity to better understand how to capture sights, sounds, and feelings in words.**

Major Concepts

* Everyone can write poems. (page 177)
* Writers of poetry are also readers of poetry. (page 178)
* Poetry looks and sounds different from prose. (page 179)
* Free verse uses lines of any length, without any set measure. (page 180)
* Students can use clusters or lists to gather ideas for poems. (page 181)
* Repetition and comparison add special touches to poetry. (pages 182-183)

Planning Notes

Materials Needed: Have a diverse collection of poems in the classroom. Quotes about poetry posted on classroom walls are also effective, as are poetry listening centers. In the listening center, have recorded poems and written copies for each selection.

School and Community Uses: Blitz the school with poetry. Here's how: Have children make copies of their favorite poems. The night before a "poetry blitz" have groups of parent volunteers tape the poems in appropriate places throughout the school (the hallways, waiting rooms, the office). Children will have fun reading these poems all day.

Writing Other Forms of Poetry

(pages 184-189)

When we offer children traditional and invented poetic forms, as we do in *Writing Other Forms of Poetry*, we offer children what Gregory Denman (Heinemann 1988) calls "the poet's invisible hand." We give students structures upon which they can build their own ideas.

This chapter teaches students about three traditional forms: cinquain, limerick, and haiku. Then students are invited to write haiku. Invented poetry comes next, with examples of alphabet poetry, concrete poetry, and Five W's poetry. The chapter ends with a simple way to write a Five W's poem.

Rationale

● **Research has shown that young children enjoy traditional poetry with its rhyme, rhythms, and structure.**

● **As students work with haiku, they learn to refine observation and to express feeling *through* the descriptions.**

● **Haiku, with its 17-syllable limitation, challenges writers to be both descriptive and suggestive.**

● **Writing limericks, a favorite form among children, is of great value in developing word choice, sentence structure, and humor.**

Major Concepts

* Traditional forms of poetry include, among others, cinquain, haiku, and limerick, which all include the writer's perspective. (page 185)

* Haiku attempts to links nature and the seasons to human nature. (pages 186-187)

* Short forms of poetry require exact word choice. (page 187)

* "Invented Poetry" demonstrates that English is a living language. (pages 188-189)

Planning Notes

Materials Needed: You will need many books of poetry in your classroom. You may want to make poetry anthologies, so paper, metal rings, and other bookmaking supplies are in order.

Reading/Listening/Thinking Connections: We must never forget that poetry began as a spoken art. Poetry begs to be heard because of its inherent lyric qualities. Read poetry aloud.

The

TOOLS of Learning

"The Tools of Learning" will help students improve all of their study and learning skills. Included in this section of the handbook are chapters on reading, vocabulary, speaking, thinking, working in groups, test-taking, and much more. There are even guidelines for reading graphics and performing poems. The table of contents below lists all of the chapters in "The Tools of Learning" section of the handbook. The page numbers refer to the location of each chapter summary in this guide.

Special Note: For minilessons related to tools of learning, see pages 120-125.

Improving Your Reading

Improving Vocabulary and Spelling

Improving Speaking and Listening

Improving Your Thinking

Improving Your Learning Skills

Reading Graphics

(pages 193-197)

"Reading graphics" means understanding symbols, diagrams, tables, and other kinds of pictorial information. Graphics are among the oldest forms of written communication. Our first written languages used graphics, not letters or words.

Reading Graphics explains symbols, diagrams, and tables. The chapter begins by explaining that graphics are informational, not merely decorative. The next four pages explore the three types of graphics in detail, along with examples and tips for understanding each.

Rationale

- **Students need to know how to understand common graphics found in classroom materials, in public information, and in different media.**

- **The skills needed to "read" graphics and other visual forms of information differ from those needed to read verbal information.**

Major Concepts

* Graphics give information and help students learn. (page 193)

* Symbols are simple graphics that stand for something. (page 194)

* Diagrams are graphics that show the parts of something, or how something works. (page 195)

* Tables are graphics that organize numbers and words to give information quickly. (page 196)

* Tables can be used to show many kinds of information, including schedules, menus, and more. (page 197)

Planning Notes

Materials Needed: Collect examples of graphics (especially symbols) from magazines, newspapers, and classroom materials. Have ready a photograph of a telephone (perhaps in a dictionary or an encyclopedia).

Using Strategies to Read New Words

(pages 198-199)

Words are the building blocks of reading and writing. To learn to read and write, children need to recognize and spell the most common words quickly and automatically. They also need to develop strategies for recognizing "hard words" that, at first, they cannot pronounce.

Using Strategies to Read New Words presents four plans for tackling difficult words: "Read, guess, and check"; "Look for word parts you do know"; "Look for prefixes, suffixes, and roots"; and "Look for compound words." At the end of the chapter, children are reminded to ask for help if none of these strategies work.

Rationale

● **Word recognition is an important part of the comprehension process.**

● **Students need strategies to read new words.**

Major Concepts

✱ Students can use the "read, guess, and check" strategy (context clues) to read new words. (page 198)

✱ Looking for *smaller words* and *common patterns* within "difficult" words is useful. (page 199)

✱ Recognizing and using roots, prefixes, and suffixes to break a long word into smaller parts is also useful. (page 199)

✱ Looking for compound words is another strategy to simplify reading longer words. (page 199)

Planning Notes

Materials Needed: Children need opportunities to apply the word-recognition strategies they are learning throughout the school day. Here are two teaching strategies adapted from *Classrooms That Work: They All Read and Write* by Patricia Cunningham and Michael Allington (Harper Collins 1994).

Big Word Boards: The authors suggest using *Big Word Boards*—bulletin boards listing big words that are keys to understanding a unit of study. Begin by identifying 15-20 "big words" you want to highlight. Write them on index cards, and each day add four or five to the bulletin board. As you do, spell them out loud (let students do the same, with and without looking), look at word parts together, and discuss or mention these words again as they occur in lectures, films, experiments, or discussions.

You Be the Expert: The authors also suggest a vocabulary-building/word-recognition strategy that puts children at the center of the teaching/learning process. Many children have a hobby or a passion for a certain topic (for example, baseball cards, trains, their culture). They often know a lot about the meaning, pronunciation, and spelling of words specific to that topic. Allot time each week for your experts to share what they've learned, including new words.

Reading to Understand

(pages 200-205)

Reading comprehension is the process of making meaning from a text. It is a complex and interactive process—involving the readers' abilities to build upon their own knowledge and skills when they meet new concepts and information. In a sense, the more students know *before* they read, the more they will be able to understand *when* they read. Strengthening reading comprehension involves building background knowledge about the concepts that students will be meeting in their reading.

Reading to Understand offers students tools or strategies for becoming interactive, thoughtful readers. The chapter begins with a plan of action: read often, read a lot of different things, change your speed as you read, and use reading strategies. The last item on the list, "use reading strategies," comprises most of the chapter's content. Students will find an explanation of several strategies to use before, during, and after reading.

Rationale

● **Students need strategies to help them become more active and thoughtful readers.**

● **Students in the middle elementary grades need ways to unlock the structure of non-fiction texts, which are often introduced at this time.**

● **Many students are capable readers, but, at times, they do not carry out their reading tasks in an efficient manner. For example, they may spend too much time decoding proper nouns, or neglect to vary their reading speed.**

Major Concepts

✳ To read is to understand, learn, remember, and discover. (page 200)

✳ There are several ways students can improve their reading. (page 200)

✳ Strategies are tools for reading effectively and efficiently. (page 201)

✳ Reading strategies can be modeled/taught/learned in the context of classroom reading instruction. (pages 202-205)

Building Vocabulary Skills

(pages 207-213)

Students need a strong vocabulary to understand what they read and hear, and to express themselves in writing and speaking. The good news is that children have been learning new words almost since they were born.

Building Vocabulary Skills begins with basic concepts. The introduction notes that students see and hear new words all the time, and that they will benefit from making these new words part of their vocabularies. The rest of the chapter explains seven strategies students can use to learn new words: read a lot, use context clues, keep a new-word notebook, practice using new words, use a dictionary, use a thesaurus, and use word parts.

Rationale

● **A strong vocabulary is fundamental to all language skills.**

● **Giving students several ways to learn new words equips them with the tools they need to build a strong vocabulary.**

● **Giving students a variety of word-learning strategies encourages them to be independent learners.**

Major Concepts

✱ The more words students know, the better they can express their thoughts and feelings. (page 207)

✱ The best way to learn new words is to read a lot. (page 208)

✱ Nearby words can help students figure out the meaning of a new word. (page 208)

✱ Dictionaries and thesauruses can help students learn new words. (pages 210-212)

✱ Dividing a word into parts (prefixes, suffixes, roots) can help students understand what the word means. (page 213)

Planning Notes

Materials Needed: You'll need supplies for your students to make new-word notebooks and several copies of a dictionary and thesaurus.

Dictionary of Prefixes, Suffixes, and Roots

(pages 214-223)

Vocabulary building is a key element in a student's growth as a reader and as an independent learner. Research has shown that memorization of vocabulary lists is an inefficient and inadequate method for enriching vocabulary. What does work is to tap into a student's natural curiosity about language.

The **Dictionary of Prefixes, Suffixes, and Roots** helps students learn about language in general and figure out the meanings of specific new words. The chapter includes lists of common prefixes, suffixes, and roots. Each word part is defined and used in a word.

Rationale

- **Vocabulary knowledge is fundamental to reading comprehension.**

- **Becoming aware of and understanding the meanings of word parts (prefixes, suffixes, and roots) helps students figure out the meanings of new words.**

Major Concepts

* Prefixes are word parts that come at the beginning of a word, before the root. (pages 215-216)

* Suffixes are word parts that come at the end of a word, after the root. (pages 217-218)

* A root is the main part of a word. It helps you understand the word's meaning. (pages 219-223)

Planning Notes

Chapter Links: The following chapters in the handbook will help students better understand the value of the "Dictionary of Prefixes, Suffixes, and Roots":

* "Building Vocabulary Skills," pages 207-213
* "Using Strategies to Read New Words," pages 198-199

Becoming a Better Speller

(pages 224-227)

"Spelling as a subject ranks just below reading and mathematics as a national priority," wrote Donald Graves in *Writing: Teachers & Children at Work*. Graves was referring to a national survey of parents. We, too, feel that spelling is important, but not as an end unto itself. Rather, spelling instruction needs to be integrated with learning to read and write.

In general, we want students to spell an ever-growing number of words correctly and automatically when they write. In rough drafts or journal entries, we want students to take risks with words they say but aren't sure how to spell. We also want students to learn how to find the correct spelling of a word. And when they are proofreading, we hope our students care about spelling for the correct reason: readability of their work.

When they are reading, we want students to notice common letter patterns and the positional constraints of some letters and letter clusters. We want them to recognize and understand new words derived from common roots they know. We hope, too, that they will analogize to pronounce unknown words, and that they will become sensitive to how words look on the page.

Becoming a Better Speller is a self-help guide for students. The chapter discusses five ways to become a better speller: making a spelling dictionary, using a sensory strategy to remember spellings, using sayings and acrostics to remember spellings, proofreading for spelling, and learning some basic spelling rules.

Rationale

- **Spelling is an important aspect of the writing and communicating process.**
- **Students learn to spell as they read and write, not just when they take tests.**
- **The more experience students have with words, the better spellers they will be.**

Major Concepts

* Many "new" words are related to words students already know how to spell. (page 224)
* There are strategies students can use to become better spellers. (pages 225-227)
* It helps to use all the senses when learning to spell. (page 225)
* Knowing a few basic rules can help students avoid common errors. (page 227)

A History of the English Language

(pages 228-231)

A common ancestor of English and many other languages is the **Indo-European language.** It was spoken in east-central Europe more than 5,000 years ago. Modern languages stemming from Indo-European, including English, Spanish, German, and French, share many similar words. *Differences* in languages arose when speakers of Indo-European broke up into smaller groups and migrated throughout Europe and Asia.

A History of the English Language takes readers back more than 2,000 years to a period when the Celts lived in Britain. It traces the development of the English language and reminds us that our language will continue to change and grow. The chapter ends with a list of English words borrowed from other languages.

Rationale

● **Children are interested in the origins of their language.**

● **Understanding the origin of language can help students appreciate the power of words.**

● **This chapter may encourage students to learn more about the history of English, or the history of other languages.**

Major Concepts

✱ English is related to other languages. (page 228)

✱ The earliest form of English was spoken by the Celts living in Britain. (page 228)

✱ English continues to evolve. (page 230)

✱ Many English words come from around the world. (page 231)

Planning Notes

Materials Needed: Globe or world map, chalkboard or overhead.

Reading/Writing Connections: Trace words that interest your class. To begin, look at the handbook's sample dictionary page (page 211) and find where word histories (origins) are noted. Then look for word histories in your classroom dictionary. Words from other languages, such as

"a la mode," "fiesta," "prima donna," and "piano," are particularly interesting to look up.

School and Community Uses: This chapter lends itself to an interpretive reading. Students could also create a historical background mural based on the information presented in this chapter.

Learning to View

(pages 233-237)

Television plays a major role in shaping what children know and believe about the world. Some students spend as much time watching TV as they do in school! This means that children need to become educated viewers of television.

Learning to View begins by acknowledging that, while many people hold a negative view of TV, there are worthwhile programs. Television allows children to see and learn about people, places, and events that they could never see in person. This chapter helps students become better consumers of news programs, specials, and commercials.

Rationale

- **Most students are unaware of the power and influence of TV.**
- **Students need to become critical viewers of TV.**
- **Students will learn more from TV specials if they follow a few active-viewing guidelines.**

Major Concepts

* Some people feel that TV is "bad," but there are many worthwhile educational programs on TV. (page 233)

* TV news doesn't show everything that happens, but it should give all the basic facts for events it covers. (page 234)

* Students can learn a lot from TV specials by viewing them thoughtfully and actively. (page 235)

* TV commercials have a goal: to get people to buy things. Commercials use many special techniques to accomplish this goal. (pages 236-237)

Learning to Listen

(pages 238-239)

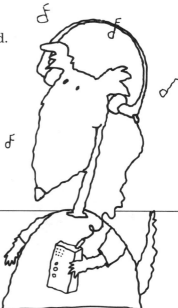

Students spend more time listening than they do speaking, reading, and writing combined. With that much "practice," you might expect students to develop good listening skills automatically. But, of course, they don't. Students become good listeners by working at it.

Learning to Listen emphasizes that listening is more than just hearing. It is a process that involves the mind as well as the ears. The checklist of good listening skills provides specific tips for effective listening.

Rationale

- **Many students are unaware of the difference between hearing and listening.**

- **Good listening skills help students learn more and learn faster.**

- **Good listening skills help students become more successful, not only in the classroom, but also in their personal relationships and in their lives outside school.**

Major Concepts

* Listening is different from hearing; it involves paying attention and thinking about what is being said. (page 238)

* Listening is a learning skill; the better a student listens, the more he or she will learn. (page 238)

* Good listeners use their eyes as well as their ears. (page 239)

* Good listeners are active listeners. They listen for key words and phrases, ask questions, and take notes. (page 239)

Performing Poems

(pages 240-245)

When poetry moves from the page to the stage, we call it poetry performance. Students get on their feet, individually and in teams, to present poetry on stage or in an open space.

Performing Poems opens with third-grader Lola and her classmates watching a poetry presentation at their school. They're having so much fun, they want to perform themselves. The rest of the chapter outlines five steps in the performance process: form a team, find a poem, script the poem, score the poem, and perform the poem. The chapter ends with an invitation to score and perform "What Is a Poem" by Allan Wolf.

Rationale

● **To bring poetry to life, children read, hear, and speak poetry.**

● **Performance encourages cooperative learning.**

● **Presenting poems gives students a sense of purpose.**

● **As students take their performance elsewhere, they learn how to conduct themselves in front of groups.**

Major Concepts

✱ Poetry performance is fun. (page 240)

✱ Many poems can be scripted and scored. (pages 242-243)

✱ Here are five tips for performing poems: act confident, face your audience, name the poem, use an "outside" voice, and exit quietly. (page 244)

Planning Notes

Materials Needed: Collect as many poetry books as possible and have them available in the classroom. A tape recorder comes in handy for those interested in hearing and revising their performance voices.

Reading/Writing Connections: Learning poems for performance requires repeated readings, which helps young readers acquire word recognition skills. Also, when children score *collaboratively*, as suggested in this chapter, it gives them the chance to discuss alternative meanings.

Across-the-Curriculum Possibilities: There are many poetry books for use with content-area material. Here are a few outstanding content-area collections with many good performance pieces: *Where Fish Go in Winter: And Answers To Other Great Mysteries* by Amy Koss (Price, Stern, Sloan 1987); *Creatures of Earth, Sea, and Sky* by Georgia Heard (Boyds Mills Press 1992); *Dinosaur Dances* by Jane Yolen (G.P. Putnam's Sons 1990); *Click, Rumble, Roar: Poems About Machines* selected by Lee Bennett Hopkins (Thomas Y. Crowell 1987).

School and Community Uses: Your class can give other classes a five-minute "poetry break." A "poetry break" is a short presentation that can come any time during the day. Arrange for your students to visit other rooms with the intention of performing one poem. A poster labeled "Poetry Break" would be a fun prop to hold up as they enter the classroom they're visiting.

Giving Short Talks

(pages 246-251)

Giving Short Talks will help third graders become more comfortable with public speaking—a lifelong skill. This chapter explains step-by-step how to prepare and present a short talk.

Giving Short Talks begins by letting students know that at first everybody finds it scary to speak in front of a group. But public speaking becomes easier with practice. The following pages take students through the process of preparing and giving a short talk. Finally, a student model about skunks is included.

Rationale

● **Practice in public speaking builds a lifelong skill.**

● **Preparing and presenting a talk step-by-step teaches students that big assignments are easier when they're divided into smaller tasks.**

● **Students develop skills (such as choosing a topic and gathering and organizing information) used in other assignments.**

Major Concepts

＊ Speaking in front of a group can be scary, but it becomes easier with practice. (page 246)

＊ Preparing and giving a short talk can be divided into seven steps. (pages 247-250)

Planning Notes

Materials Needed: Have a supply of note cards on hand. If available, an audio- or videotape recorder can help students practice and polish their talks.

Reading/Writing Connections: Students may use previously completed written reports as the basis for short talks. This will give them extra oral-presentation practice. It will also help them see the differences between a good written report and a good talk.

Across-the-Curriculum Possibilities: Almost any content area can provide material for short talks. Having students think about topics from different content areas is a good way to help them understand the different purposes for talks. For example, a talk about science is more likely to have the purpose of helping listeners learn something new, while a talk about social studies is more likely to have the purpose of sharing important details about an event.

School and Community Uses: Encourage your students to put their public speaking skills to use outside of the classroom. They may present their talks to clubs they belong to or at a PTA event.

Learning to Interview

(pages 252-255)

Interviewing gets students actively involved in the information gathering process. When students conduct interviews, they are practicing very important skills: getting organized, speaking, listening, note taking, and thinking clearly.

Learning to Interview begins with an example of a third grader's assignment and a brief definition of an interview. This is followed by strategies for planning and carrying out an interview. The chapter ends with an interview in action: student questions, recorded answers, and an interview report.

Rationale

● **Conducting an interview shows students that the spoken word can be a valuable source of information and learning.**

● **The interview process helps students develop listening and speaking skills.**

Major Concepts

✱ An interview is another way to gather information. (page 252)

✱ Students need to carefully plan and prepare for an interview. (page 253)

✱ Students need to be polite and alert during the interview. (page 254)

✱ Information from interviews can be written in an interesting form. (page 255)

Planning Notes

Materials Needed: Have on hand interviews from newspapers or magazines (*Horn Book, Instructor*) as well as books that incorporate information from interviews, such as biographies by Pamela Dell. A tape recorder would be useful.

Reading/Writing Connections: As you discuss interview reports, ask students to imagine the questions that might have been asked. Also point out how direct quotations are used in the writing.

Across-the-Curriculum Possibilities: The content areas provide infinite interview possibilities. Bring experts into the classroom whenever possible, and let your students interview them. Class field trips provide natural connections with experts, too. The information gleaned can be used in articles, books, and projects your students are working on.

School and Community Uses: Arrange interviews with school personnel that work behind the scenes—secretaries, custodians, and so on. Find outlets for interviews and reports, such as the school newspaper, person-of-the-week announcements, posters placed in hallways, etc.

Telling Stories

(pages 256-261)

Storytelling is as old as society itself. People from around the world have always told tales as a way of passing down their beliefs, history, and traditions to future generations. Telling stories is one of the most fundamental ways to make sense of the world and our place in it.

Telling Stories begins with an invitation to students to become their family's own storyteller. The introduction is followed by a five-step process for learning stories, which includes a note-taking strategy. The chapter ends with a sample story told by Charles Temple, a storyteller from New York who tells the tale of the "Walking Catfish."

Rationale

● **By sharing stories, children begin to develop a better understanding of themselves, their families, and their world.**

● **Telling stories improves self-esteem and builds confidence and poise for speaking in front of a group.**

● **Television has taken away the need to imagine. Teaching students how to tell stories is like a wake-up call to their creative imaginations.**

● **The memorization process gives story mapping a functional purpose.**

● **As students support each other's efforts to be successful, storytelling improves class cooperation.**

Major Concepts

✱ Telling stories is an age-old tradition. (page 256)

✱ Folktales, fairy tales, legends, and tall tales are all fun to tell. (page 257)

✱ Students can learn to tell stories using a five-step process. (page 257)

Planning Notes

Materials Needed: Have books of folktales and fairy tales in your classroom. The popular book *Children Tell Stories: A Teaching Guide* by Martha Hamilton & Mitch Weiss (Richard Owen 1990) has an appendix with 25 stories for children to tell. Also have index cards and a tape recorder available.

Reading/Speaking Connections: Once students catch on to storytelling, everything they read turns into a potential storytelling source. Great storytellers remind us to look for humorous or interesting material in newspaper articles and letters.

Across-the-Curriculum Possibilities: "Community" is an important theme in many third-grade classrooms. Stories are an essential part of any community. Encourage students to find and share community stories as part of their work in social studies.

School and Community Uses: If possible, videotape your students so their stories can be shared with other classes and within the community. Each student could illustrate his or her tale and prepare a picture book to accompany the taped version.

Getting Organized

(pages 263-267)

Everyone would agree that helping students collect, arrange, and use information is a primary goal of education. The challenge, of course, is how to help them do this. We can, among other things, introduce them to reading and thinking strategies as well as to writing-to-learn techniques.

Getting Organized will acquaint students with valuable ways to gather and arrange facts and details using graphic organizers. This chapter gives examples of five types of organizers, each one offering students a different way to collect and organize their ideas.

Rationale

- Graphic organizers help students organize thoughts and information.
- Students need to practice using graphic organizers for gathering and remembering details, getting facts straight, and arranging information.

Major Concepts

* Being organized is a key to success. (page 263)
* Graphic organizers help learners gather and group ideas. (page 263)
* Different graphic organizers serve different purposes. (pages 263-267)

Thinking Clearly

(pages 268-273)

Thinking clearly helps people succeed. It helps attorneys present convincing cases. It helps mechanics repair engines. It helps coaches plan effective strategies for upcoming games. And it helps young learners become more successful in almost everything they do—inside and outside of school.

Thinking Clearly begins with an attention-grabbing scenario—a school-aged child in a mall loses track of her mother. The chapter then shows how to solve problems (like being lost in a mall), how to make decisions, and how to use facts and opinions correctly. The last two pages discuss four points to remember about stating facts.

Rationale

● **Students need to learn the thinking skills required to solve problems and make decisions.**

● **Students need to understand the difference between facts and opinions.**

● **Students need to know how to use facts and opinions correctly in their writing and speaking, and to be aware of how others use facts and opinions.**

Major Concepts

✱ Thinking clearly is a skill that students can learn. (page 268)

✱ Students can learn to solve problems, step-by-step. (page 269)

✱ Students can use clear thinking to help them make decisions. (page 270)

✱ It's important to understand the difference between facts and opinions. (page 271)

Writing to Learn Math

(pages 274-275)

Educators are increasingly aware of the many connections between language and mathematics. Writing about math helps students discover and reinforce what they know about math.

Writing to Learn Math helps students see that writing down their thoughts and questions is part of the process of learning new math concepts. The chapter explains that learning logs are a good way for students to write about what they have learned and about what they don't understand yet. The chapter provides strategies for writing different types of entries in math learning logs.

Rationale

- **Writing is an important part of learning math.**
- **Learning to write reflectively in a math log broadens students' understanding of concepts, helping them identify and reinforce what they know.**

Major Concepts

* In math logs, students can record what they do day by day and what they have learned, as well as questions about what they don't understand. (page 274)

* There are strategies to help students find the kind of math-log entries that will work best for them. (page 275)

Planning Notes

Materials Needed: Students will need a notebook (or a section of a notebook) in which to keep their writing about math. Keeping their math writing together reinforces an organizational skill necessary to good study habits. Students will also benefit from looking over their math-journal entries.

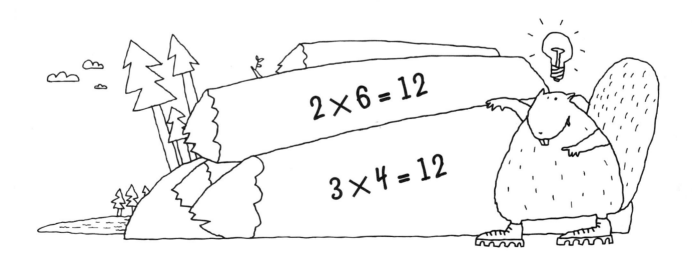

Completing Assignments

(pages 277-279)

Learning to complete assignments means learning to plan ahead. Mastering this skill will enable students to break big tasks into manageable parts, learn from their assignments, and do their best work.

Completing Assignments begins by emphasizing the importance of planning ahead. There's one list of tips telling how to *plan ahead*, and another list of tips telling how to *do the work*. The chapter concludes with a sample daily assignment chart and a sample plan for a big (long-range) assignment. These charts show how students can put their plans on paper.

Rationale

● **Third graders do get assignments that will take them a few days or a week to complete.**

● **Learning to plan their time and complete long-range assignments is a valuable life skill.**

● **Learning to complete assignments gives students a sense of confidence and competence.**

Major Concepts

* Planning ahead is a big part of completing assignments successfully. (page 277)

* There are strategies students can use to help them complete their assignments. (page 278)

* There are forms students can use to write down their plans for daily assignments and big assignments. (page 279)

Planning Notes

School and Community Uses: Parents can help reinforce what their children are learning in school about planning ahead and completing assignments. You may want to show parents page 278 of the handbook. This will give you an opportunity to discuss issues such as the student's need for a quiet place to study, and the best time to do homework (often *not* right after school).

Working in Groups

(pages 280-283)

Some things can only be accomplished by students working in cooperation with others—putting on a play, for example. And some things are better *learned* by working with others—such as the multiplication table. But students need a few basic skills to work with others successfully.

Working in Groups points out that there are many activities that require people to work together, and that groups come in all different sizes. The chapter also offers tips for working in pairs and in small groups. There is an outline of a group plan that students can use as a framework for their own plans.

Rationale

● **Working in groups allows students to do things they couldn't do alone.**

● **Knowing how to work as a member of a group is an important life skill.**

● **Students need to learn basic teamwork skills, such as listening, sharing, and compromising.**

Major Concepts

✳ Some things can only be accomplished by people working together in groups. (page 280)

✳ Two people who work together are called partners. (page 281)

✳ Working in a group requires listening to others and sharing ideas and jobs. (page 282)

✳ Every group project should include a plan. (page 283)

Taking Tests

(pages 284-291)

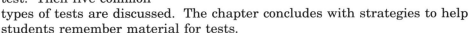

Tests are an inescapable part of school, and, for some, not always a pleasant part. Yet tests are an important way for both teachers and students to assess how they're doing.

Taking Tests begins with the assurance that tests are not a problem if students keep up with their class work and study effectively. The chapter offers "Five Smart Things to Do" to prepare for any kind of test. Then five common types of tests are discussed. The chapter concludes with strategies to help students remember material for tests.

Rationale

● **Tests are one way to measure learning about a subject.**

● **Understanding how to prepare for and take various kinds of tests empowers students.**

Major Concepts

* Tests are not a problem if students keep up with their class work and study. (page 284)

* There are things students can do to prepare for any kind of test. (page 285)

* There are strategies students can use to do their best on objective and short-answer tests. (pages 286-290)

* There are strategies students can use to remember material for tests. (page 291)

Planning Notes

Testing Situations: Using this section will depend upon the types of tests you plan to (or must) give your students. Before giving a test, teach or review the strategies that relate to that type of test.

Handbook

MINILESSONS

Minilessons can transform any classroom into an active learning environment. (We define a minilesson as instruction that lasts about 10-15 minutes and covers a single idea or a core of basic information.) Minilessons can be delivered from the front of the room and include the entire class. They can also be individualized or implemented in writing groups. Ideally, each lesson will address a specific need your students have at a particular time. This makes the lesson meaningful and successful.

In this section, there is at least one minilesson listed for each chapter in the handbook. You will find this section invaluable when planning activities related to the handbook.

The Process of Writing

"There's nothing I like better!" ...... *All About Writing*

READ page 13 in your handbook. It tells how one student feels about writing. Now **WRITE** a few sentences that tell how you feel about writing. You can write whatever you want to. Be honest!

Follow the Dotted Line .... *All About Writing*

OPEN your handbook to pages 14 and 15. After you read these pages, **LIST** the five steps in the writing process. (To find the five steps, follow the dotted lines from one circle to the next.) Then **WRITE** one sentence about each step.

Made by Peter .... *One Writer's Process*

READ the chapter called "One Writer's Process." It begins on page 16. Then **COMPLETE** the following sentences by adding one or two ideas. Use your own words. The first sentence has been done for you.

1. During prewriting, Peter picked a subject and collected details .

2. When Peter wrote his first draft, he _____
   _____ .

3. When Peter revised his draft, he _____
   _____ .

4. During editing and proofreading, Peter _____
   _____ .

5. When Peter published his story, he _____ .

Getting to Know PC . . . . *Writing with a Computer*

TURN to pages 20 and 21 in your handbook. **STUDY** the computer pictured on these two pages. Then **COVER UP** the names of the different parts; see if you can name the parts just by looking at the picture.

The Name Game . . . . *Writing with a Computer*

OPEN your handbook to page 24. Have your teacher or a parent show you where to put your fingers on the "home row" of the keyboard. **PRACTICE** keyboarding your name until you can do it quickly.

Saving the Best . . . . *Planning Portfolios*

READ page 26 in your handbook. **NAME** one of your favorite pieces of writing. Then **WRITE** a few sentences explaining why you might want to save it in a portfolio.

The Last Step, the Best Step . . . . *Publishing Your Writing*

REVIEW the chapter called "Publishing Your Writing." It starts on page 30. **LIST** the different ways you have published your own writing. Then **WRITE DOWN** one or two new publishing ideas that you would like to try. **SHARE** your ideas with a classmate.

Group Authors . . . . *Publishing Your Writing*

PLAN a publishing project with a small group of classmates. You could make a book that includes a story by each group member. Or you could all perform one story or poem. It's up to your group. **REVIEW** "Five Cool Publishing Ideas" on page 31 for help.

Good News, Bad News . . . . *Building a File of Writing Ideas*

TURN to page 37 in your handbook and **READ** number 3. Then **START** a list of your bests, worsts, and favorites in a writing notebook or folder. **KEEP** adding ideas during the year.

The Road of Life . . . . *Building a File of Writing Ideas*

OPEN your handbook to page 36. **STUDY** the model life map. **PLAN** your own life map by listing events you would like to include on it. You may have to ask your parents for help with early events. Then **DECIDE** how you would like your map to look. (Later, you can draw your map to display in the room.)

5 × W = 5 W's . . . . *Collecting Details*

READ page 39 in your handbook. **THINK** of an experience you would like to write about. **WRITE** it at the top of a sheet of paper. On the same sheet, **LIST** the 5 W's: Who? What? When? Where? and Why? **SKIP** two lines between each question. Then **ANSWER** each question about your experience.

Using Your Senses . . . . *Collecting Details*

READ "Study Your Subject" on page 39. Then **THINK** of a place, an object, or an event that you would like to visit. **WRITE** it on the top of a sheet of paper. **LIST** the following questions under your subject. **LEAVE** space between each one.

1. How does (or did) it look?
2. How does it sound?
3. How does it taste?
4. How does it smell?
5. How does it feel?

Now **ANSWER** as many of these questions as you can about your subject.

Point by Point . . . . *Planning and Drafting Guide*

READ page 40 in your handbook. **LIST** *subject, purpose, form* and *readers* on a separate piece of paper. **WRITE** down the four key points for a subject of your choice—a personal story, a play, a poem, a report, or so on. **USE** the model in the handbook as a guide.

Start with a Bang . . . . *Planning and Drafting Guide*

TURN to page 41 in your handbook and **READ** "Plan your beginning." Then **FIND** two beginnings in the handbook models that you really like. **SHARE** your discoveries with a classmate. **EXPLAIN** why you like each one.

Show me! . . . . *Revising Your Writing*

READ page 46 in your handbook. Then **REWRITE** each of the following sentences so they show instead of tell. One sentence has been done for you.

1. My neighbor is old.

   My neighbor has white hair and a wrinkled face.

2. We were happy.

   _____

   _____

3. We were sad.

   _____

   _____

4. Our classroom is interesting.

   _____

   _____

First You, Then Me . . . . *Conferencing with Partners*

REVIEW the handbook chapter called "Conferencing with Partners." It begins on page 48. **PRETEND** that your teacher has asked you to write a poem about something scary. **HELP** a partner decide what to write about. Also **HELP** your partner think of some good scary words to use in his or her poem. Then **TRADE** jobs. Next **ASK** your partner to help *you*—but this time pretend you are writing a silly poem.

Two heads are better than one. . . . . *Editing and Proofreading*

SELECT an editing partner. (Each of you should have a piece of writing ready.) Now **OPEN** your handbooks to page 53. **USE** the "Editing and Proofreading Checklist" to edit your own work while your partner does the same. Then exchange papers and **CHECK** each other's writing for errors.

Topic Sentence . . . . *Writing Paragraphs*

READ pages 56 and 57 in your handbook. Pay special attention to the part about topic sentences at the top of page 57. Now **TURN** to the model paragraphs on pages 58-61. Read the topic sentence for each one. On the lines below, **FILL IN** the subject and the focus for each topic sentence. The first one has been done for you.

	subject	focus
p. 58, "Cooking with Grandma"	grandma & I	cooked in the backyard
p. 59, "Zev's Deli"		
p. 60, "Living with a Little Brother"		
p. 61, "No Way to Go!"		

Types of Paragraphs . . . . *Writing Paragraphs*

REVIEW pages 58-61 in your handbook. Then **MATCH** each type of paragraph with the correct description listed below. The first one has been done for you.

Types of Paragraphs

___b___ 1. expository   a. tells a story

_____ 2. narrative   b. explains something

_____ 3. descriptive   c. tries to get readers to agree

_____ 4. persuasive   d. describes a person, place, or thing

"Amazing Hawks" . . . . *Writing a Summary*

REVIEW pages 64-66 in your handbook. Now **TURN** to page 145 and **READ** the student model report. **LIST** the main ideas that you find in the model. The ideas in your list could be used to write a summary. (You should find four to six.) **SHARE** your list with a classmate.

I smell a skunk. . . . . *Writing a Summary*

READ the model on page 251 and **LIST** the main ideas that you find in this writing. If you need help, **TURN** to page 66.
Special Challenge: **WRITE** a summary of "Skunks" using the ideas in your list.

Buggy Sentences . . . . *Writing Basic Sentences*

REVIEW page 70 in the handbook. **WRITE** this sentence at the top of a sheet of paper: I play tag. Then **REWRITE** the sentence using a different subject. **ASK** a partner to rewrite the sentence with still another subject. Next, **REWRITE** the sentence using a different verb. (You may change other words, too.) **KEEP** trading back and forth, writing sentences with different subjects and predicates. **ADD** describing words to make your sentences even more fun.

EXAMPLE SENTENCES:

Tim plays tag.   (different subject)

My sister plays tag.   (different subject)

My sister wins at tag!   (different verb)

My silly sister really likes tackle tag. (describing words plus different verb)

Neat and Complete . . . . *Writing Basic Sentences*

REVIEW the information on sentence fragments on page 71. Then **MAKE** each fragment below into a complete sentence. The first one has been done for you.

1. After the rain.   We collected worms after the rain.

2. Worked before lunch. _____

3. At the mall. _____

4. Stayed overnight. _____

5. With my best friend. _____

And Then . . . And Then . . . . *Combining Sentences*

WRITE about something you did during recess. **USE** a lot of "and's" in your writing. (*Joe ran out for a pass* and *waved his arms* and *yelled* and *then* . . .) **SWITCH** papers with a partner and **CORRECT** each other's rambling ideas. **SEE** the information about rambling sentences on page 71 for help.

People Watching .... *Combining Sentences*

COMBINE each pair of sentences below into one sentence. **USE** page 73 in your handbook to help you. The first one has been done for you.

1. Sam likes pineapple pizza. Dave likes pineapple pizza.

   Sam and Dave like pineapple pizza.

2. They made their own pizza. They made it yesterday.

   _____

3. Sam spread the dough. Sam poured on the sauce.

   _____

4. Dave chopped the pineapple. Dave sprinkled it on the pizza.

   _____

Let's eat! .... *Combining Sentences*

WRITE three sentence describing your favorite food. Then **COMBINE** all three sentences into one sentence. Look at page 73 in your handbook, "Combine with a Series," for help.

The Forms of Writing

It's my life! . . . . *Writing in Journals*

READ page 78 in your handbook. Then **WRITE** the first entry in your own personal journal. Write about something you saw, something you did, or something you heard about. Don't worry about spelling every word right. Just get all of your ideas on paper.

The Two R's: Reading and Writing *Writing in Journals*

READ page 79 in your handbook. Now **TURN** to page 260 and **READ** the story "Walking Catfish." **WRITE** a few sentences telling what you think about this story. This could be the beginning of your own reading journal.

Spot & Me . . . . *Making Albums*

OPEN your handbook to pages 82 and 83. **SELECT** a subject for a pet or best friend album. (If you make an album about a person, you could give it to him or her as a special gift.) **MAKE** some notes about what you would put in the album. **USE** the list under number 2 on page 83 for ideas.

Collecting Ideas . . . . *Writing Lists*

READ "Collecting Ideas for Writing" on page 85. On a sheet of paper, **NAME** your favorite or your worst day of the week. **LIST** different words that come to mind when you think of this day. **SHARE** your list with a classmate, and **SAVE** it in a notebook or folder. Sometime you might want to write a "day" story or poem.

Happy thoughts to you! . . . . *Writing Lists*

READ page 86 in your handbook. Then **MAKE** your own "happy list."
KEEP your list in an idea notebook, writing folder, or journal. (You may want to work on this with a partner.)

Notes to you! . . . . *Writing Friendly Notes*

REVIEW the chapter on pages 88-91 called "Writing Friendly Notes." It gives four reasons to send notes. (The red triangles point to the four reasons.) **PICK** a reason to send a note. Then **WRITE** a note to someone in your class. **ASK** the person to write back!

Five-Part Harmony . . . . *Writing Friendly Letters*

Carefully **REVIEW** page 92 in your handbook. Then **CLOSE** your handbook and **LOOK** at the list of words below. They are the parts of a friendly letter, but they are in the wrong order. **REWRITE** the list in the right order. **OPEN** your handbook to check your work.

> body
> closing
> heading
> signature
> salutation

Possum Tale . . . . *Writing Personal Narratives*

A personal narrative answers the question "Guess what happened?"
READ the personal narrative on page 97. Then **WRITE** two sentences that tell what happened. **SHARE** your ideas with a classmate.

That's strange. . . . . *Writing Personal Narratives*

On a sheet of paper, **LIST** the words *happy, funny, proud, strange,* and *important*. Under each word **WRITE** one or two things that happened to you. (List happy experiences under the word "happy" and so on.) When you finish, **ASK**, *"Which of these happenings would my classmates be most interested in?"* Then ask, *"Which of the interesting events do I remember the most about?"* This final choice would probably make a good personal narrative. For writing guidelines, see pages 98-99 in the handbook.

All in the Family . . . . *Writing Family Stories*

OPEN your handbook to pages 100-101. **READ** about family stories. Now **USE** the ideas listed on page 102 under "Read and Remember" to help you list possible subjects for your own family story. **SELECT** the best subject from your list for a story.

Knowing Your A's and B's . . . . *Writing Alphabet Books*

PRETEND that your teacher has asked you to write an alphabet book about different countries. **LIST** a country for each of the first five letters of the alphabet. The maps in your handbook (pages 353-362) will be a big help. **ADD** an interesting fact if you know one. (See the example below and the student models on page 106.)

A ustralia is a huge island known for its kangaroos _____.

B _____.

C _____.

D _____.

E _____.

Get a little crazy! . . . . *Writing Alphabet Books*

STUDY the "Next Stop" on page 109. Then **START** a zany alphabet book about food, geography, or creepy crawlers. **WRITE** at least four or five lines. **SHARE** your work. **KEEP** going if you like the start of your ABC book.

Five Easy Parts . . . . *Writing Newspaper Stories*

CUT OUT a basic news story from a newspaper. Then **OPEN** your handbook to page 111 and **REVIEW** the five parts of a news story. **LABEL** the five parts in your story. **SHARE** your work with a classmate.

Getting Down to Basics . . . . . *Writing Newspaper Stories*

On a sheet of paper, list the 5 W's (*who? what? when? where?* and *why?*). **FIND** the answers to the 5 W's for a story in a school or local newspaper. **WRITE** the answers in your own words. To show you how it's done, we've answered the 5 W's for the model news story on page 111.

Who? the students in Ms. Grayson's class

What? collected 22,000 aluminum cans

When? in six weeks

Where? mostly from their parents

Why? to raise money to buy trees for their school yard

That's interesting! . . . . *Writing Newspaper Stories*

LIST three questions to ask a classmate. As you ask the questions,
WRITE down his or her answers. (This is called interviewing.)
UNDERLINE the most interesting idea. Using this idea, **WRITE** the
first sentence of a human interest story about the classmate. (See
page 114 for a model.)

In My Opinion . . . . *Writing Newspaper Stories*

READ and **DISCUSS** the letter to the editor on page 115. Then **LIST**
three topics you would like to talk about in this type of letter.
SHARE your ideas with your classmates.

The Big Three . . . . *Writing Book Reviews*

REVIEW pages 116-117 in your handbook. On a piece of paper, **NAME**
the title of the last book you read. **ANSWER** one of the three
questions at the top of page 117 about this book. **USE** at least two or
three sentences. **SHARE** your answer with a classmate.

Book Chat . . . . *Writing Book Reviews*

READ page 116 about book reviews. Then **LIST** two or three of the best
books you have read. **SHARE** these titles with your classmates.
WRITE your next book review about a book that most of your
classmates haven't read.

The Words of Books . . . . *Writing Book Reviews*

STUDY the list of words on page 121. Then **CLOSE** your handbook and **EXPLAIN** each word listed below. When you finish, **OPEN** your handbook to check your work. The first one has been done for you.

1. Dialogue   is the talking between characters.

2. Fiction   _____

3. The plot   _____

4. The setting   _____

Why write? . . . . *Writing Business Letters*

REVIEW pages 122-123 in your handbook. **THINK** of a business letter you would like to write. Do you need or want information about something? Do you have a problem to solve? **WRITE** a sentence that tells what information you need, or what problem you have to solve.

And the Envelope, Please . . . . *Writing Business Letters*

ADDRESS an envelope to the president. (Put your return address on the envelope, too.) LOOK at page 129 in your handbook to make sure you do everything right. Here is the president's address: The President of the United States, The White House, 1600 Pennsylvania Avenue, Washington, DC 20500.

Turn left at the office. . . . . *Writing to Explain*

WRITE directions from your classroom to another part of your school. You could explain how to get to the playground, lunchroom, or library. **WRITE** your directions in a list like the one at the bottom of page 134 in your handbook. **ASK** a classmate to check your work by testing your directions.

One Way or Another . . . . *Using the Library*

REVIEW pages 137-141 in your handbook. Then **FIND OUT** if your school library uses the card catalog or a computer catalog. On a half sheet of paper, **LIST** two or three important things the handbook says about the type of catalog used in your school. **SHARE** your ideas with other members of your class.

Parts of a Book . . . . *Using the Library*

In your classroom or library, **FIND** a reference book. Then **OPEN** your handbook to "Understanding Parts of Books" on page 143. **FIND** as many of these parts as you can for the book you selected.

Getting Started . . . . *Writing Classroom Reports*

REVIEW pages 144-146 in your handbook. **CHOOSE** a subject for a classroom report. On a sheet of paper, **WRITE** at least four questions about your subject that you would like to answer. Remember to write questions that can't be answered with a *yes* or *no*.

Getting a Grip on a Grid . . . . *Writing Classroom Reports*

TURN to page 148 in your handbook and study the gathering grid. Then **MAKE** your own grid to use for a classroom report. **LEAVE** enough space for at least four questions and three sources of information. *Tip:* Use a big piece of paper for your work.

She ought to be in pictures. . . . . . . *Writing Photo Essays*

REVIEW "Writing Photo Essays" on pages 152-157. **THINK** of a person or animal that would make a good subject for this type of writing. **MAKE** a list of three or more photos you would like to take of this subject. We've started a list of photo ideas for a circus clown.

1. photo showing clown without her costume and makeup

2. photo showing clown putting on makeup

3. photo showing clown's foot next to huge clown shoe

4. _____

In the End . . . . *Writing Realistic Stories*

READ about realistic stories on pages 159-160 in the handbook. Then **THINK** of a funny, exciting, or important event in your life. **WRITE** a different ending for this experience. **SHARE** your ideas with a classmate.

You don't say. . . . . *Writing Realistic Stories*

THINK of a funny, exciting, or important event in your life. (It could be the same one you used in the last minilesson.) **WRITE** at least four lines of dialogue between two characters in your story. For help, **STUDY** the model on page 160 in your handbook.

Way Back When . . . . *Writing Time-Travel Fantasies*

READ pages 164-165 about time-travel fantasies. **PRETEND** your teacher asked you to write a fantasy about some time in the past. **DECIDE** which time you'd like to visit. **WRITE** down two or three facts that you know about this time. **SHARE** your work with a classmate.

A Problem in Time . . . . *Writing Time-Travel Fantasies*

Every good story needs a problem! **READ** the fantasy on pages 168-169 to see what we mean by a problem. **PRETEND** that you've decided to write a time-travel fantasy that takes place in outer space. **WRITE** one or two sentences describing a problem you could put in your story.

Let's Play . . . . *Writing Plays*

REVIEW pages 170-173 in your handbook about writing plays. **CHOOSE** a story that you could turn into a play. Now **LIST** the *story events*. Page 173 shows you how.

Talk! Talk! Talk! . . . . *Writing Plays*

To practice writing dialogue for a play, **START** Scene 2 for the model in the handbook (page 171). Scene 2 is described on page 173. **WORK** on this activity with a classmate if you like.

Poem Talk . . . . *Writing Free-Verse Poetry*

Do this minilesson with a partner. First **READ** pages 178 and 179 in your handbook. Then, with your partner, **PICK** a poem to read together. **TALK** about the poem. Are there **words or phrases** you like a lot? Are there **sounds** you like? How does the poem make you **feel?** **LIST** three things that you like.

"When I Grow Up" . . . . *Writing Free-Verse Poetry*

OPEN your handbook to page 180. **READ** Kristen Murphy's free-verse poem. **WRITE** the start of your own "When I Grow Up" poem. **INCLUDE** at least four things you would like to be.

Let's compare! . . . . *Writing Free-Verse Poetry*

READ about making comparisons on page 183 in your handbook. Then **READ** some of the poems in your reading book. **FIND** one example of a simile or a metaphor and one example of personification. **SHARE** your discoveries with a classmate.

All Decked Out . . . . *Writing Other Forms of Poetry*

READ about cinquain poetry on page 185 in your handbook. Then **WRITE** a **cinquain** about a favorite piece of clothing. **USE** the model in the handbook as your guide. **SHARE** your results.

The Tools of Learning

Picture Talk . . . . *Reading Graphics*

STUDY page 194 in your handbook. Then **THINK** of another symbol you know about. **MAKE** a drawing of this symbol. If you can't think of one, create a new symbol. **SHARE** your drawing with your classmates.

On the Table . . . . *Reading Graphics*

STUDY page 196 in your handbook. Then, as a class, **MAKE** your own table. Your table could tell about your favorite pets, your favorite football teams, or your favorite foods. **DRAW** a copy of this table on a large piece of paper.

Let me guess. . . . . *Using Strategies to Read New Words*

REVIEW pages 198-199 in your handbook and **PUT** a bookmark by these pages. Then **READ** about commercials on pages 236-237. **USE** the strategies on pages 198-199 to help you read any new words. **TALK** about your reading with your classmates.

I smell a skunk! . . . . *Reading to Understand*

REVIEW pages 202-203 in your handbook. Then **MAKE** your own KWL chart. On the line for the title, write "Skunks." **FILL IN** the *know* and *want* columns of your chart with ideas and questions you have about skunks. Now **READ** "Skunks" on page 251 and **FILL IN** the *learn* column of your chart.

Map It! . . . . *Reading to Understand*

READ page 204 in your handbook, and **STUDY** the model map on page 205. Now **READ** "Amazing Hawks" on page 145. **MAKE** a reading map of this model. Your map should begin with the word *hawks* in a circle. One of your main ideas could be *eating habits* or *food*.

Word Search . . . . *Building Vocabulary Skills*

TURN to page 231 in your handbook. **CHOOSE** a new word on this page to add to your vocabulary. **LOOK UP** the word in a dictionary. **LIST** three different types of information about the word (*meaning, history, synonyms,* and so on). See pages 210-211 if you're not sure how to use a dictionary.

Just the Right Word . . . . *Building Vocabulary Skills*

LOOK UP the word *run* in a thesaurus and **FIND** three synonyms for it. **WRITE** a sentence using each one. Make sure each sentence is different. See page 212 if you're not sure how to use a thesaurus.

First Cousins . . . . *Becoming a Better Speller*

OPEN your handbook to page 224 and read the first paragraph. It lists some word relatives of *night*. On a sheet of paper, **WRITE** the word *rain*. Then **WRITE** as many word relatives of *rain* as you can. **CHECK** the list of suffixes that starts on page 217 for ideas. **SHARE** your words with a classmate.

By the Rules . . . . *Becoming a Better Speller*

REVIEW page 227 in your handbook. It gives four basic spelling rules. **THINK** of at least one word that fits each rule. (Don't use the words in the handbook.) **SHARE** your words with your classmates.

New and Improved . . . . . . *A History of the English Language*

READ the "New Words" section on page 230 in the handbook. **LIST** two or three inventions that have added words to English. **THINK** of two new words related to each invention, and **WRITE** them next to the correct invention. **TALK** about your ideas with your classmates.

Seeing the World . . . . *Learning to View*

REVIEW page 233 in your handbook. **LOOK** over the list of things you can see on television. **THINK** of one person, place, or thing you saw on television that you have never seen in person. **WRITE** a few sentences about it. *What do you remember most? What did you learn? What did you like or not like about the program?*

Tell me a story. . . . . *Learning to Listen*

READ the listening tips on page 239. Then **LISTEN** carefully while a classmate tells you a personal story. **RETELL** the story in as much detail as you can. **ASK** your partner how well you did. When you finish, **SWITCH** roles.

Speaking Parts . . . . *Performing Poems*

TEAM UP with one or two classmates. **SCRIPT** one of the poems in the handbook. **OPEN** your handbook to page 242 for an example script. You could also **SCORE** the poem using the example on page 243 as a guide.

Talk Topic . . . . *Giving Short Talks*

READ the top of page 247 in the handbook. Then **LIST** these three headings on a piece of paper: *Something that happened, Something I like to do, Something I read about.* **SKIP** about four lines between each one. **WRITE** two or three topics under each heading. **SHARE** your list with a classmate. Then **SELECT** the best topic for a short talk.

Dream Job . . . . *Learning to Interview*

READ page 252 in the handbook. Then **WRITE** at the top of a piece of paper what you would like to be when you grow up. **LIST** three or four questions you would ask someone who knows about this job. **DECIDE** who you could ask these questions. **SHARE** your list with your classmates.

"Walking Catfish" . . . . *Telling Stories*

PAIR UP with a classmate. **READ** the story on pages 260-261, and **STUDY** the note cards on pages 258-259. Then **WRITE** the rest of the note cards for this story. **COMPARE** note cards with other teams.

Story Cards . . . . *Telling Stories*

REVIEW pages 257-259 in your handbook. Then **TURN** to page 160 and **READ** "A Very Far Hit." **WRITE** one note card for the first line in the story and another note card for the last line. Then **WRITE** one note card for each important event in between the beginning and the end. **SHARE** your work with your classmates.

My Best Bud . . . . *Getting Organized*

READ about a *describing wheel* at the top of page 265. Then **MAKE** a describing wheel. **PUT** the name of someone you like in the middle of the wheel. Then **FILL IN** lots of good describing words.

Circling Around the Subjects . . . . . . *Getting Organized*

REVIEW page 266 in your handbook. Then **THINK** of two animals that are alike in some ways. **MAKE** a Venn diagram comparing these animals. You can use information you know, or read about the animals in a reference book.

Trouble, Trouble . . . . *Thinking Clearly*

Do this minilesson with a partner. **PRETEND** that you are at the playground with a friend. You find a dog that can't get up. You want to help, but you don't know what to do. No one else is at the playground. **FOLLOW** the directions on page 269 to solve this problem. **WRITE** down your ideas for numbers 1-4 on this page. **SHARE** your work with your classmates.

Log It . . . . *Writing to Learn Math*

REVIEW "Writing to Learn Math" on page 274-275. Then **WRITE** a few sentences or draw a few pictures that explain something you just learned in math.

Working Smart . . . . *Completing Assignments*

THINK about how you complete assignments. Then **READ** page 278. **LIST** two or three new things you will try the next time you study. **COMPARE** lists with your classmates.

Surprise! . . . . *Working in Groups*

READ pages 280-281 with a partner. Then **PLAN** a pretend party for someone you both know and like. **FILL OUT** a planning outline like the one on page 283. **SHARE** the plan with this person.

Short Answer . . . . *Taking Tests*

REVIEW page 290 in your handbook. **THINK** about a subject you are studying in science. **WRITE DOWN** some ideas for a short-answer question about the subject. As a class, **COME UP** with a good question. Then **PLAN** and **WRITE** your answer following the tips on page 290.

The Proofreader's Guide

I love cookies. . . . . *Using Punctuation*

WRITE a paragraph about your favorite food. Write at least four sentences. Leave out the periods at the end of your sentences. Then **TRADE** paragraphs with a partner. Put periods where they are needed in each other's paragraph.

U. R. Terrific . . . . *Using Punctuation*

WRITE the first and middle initials plus the last name of each person in your family, your favorite movie or TV star, and your best friend. Be sure to use periods where they are needed.

Hungry Mungry Monkey . . . . *Using Punctuation*

PRETEND you are going to write a story about a family of monkeys. **MAKE UP** a last name for the family. Also make up first names and middle names for each of the monkeys. **WRITE OUT** the full names. Then **WRITE** the names using first and middle initials.

A catfish is smooth, shiny, and slippery! . . . . *Using Punctuation*

WRITE a sentence using three words to describe an alligator. **PUT** commas where they are needed. Now **WRITE** sentences about two other animals. Use three describing words in each sentence. Don't forget the commas!

Don't forget contractions! .... *Using Punctuation*

OPEN your handbook to page 301. Study the section on using apostrophes in contractions. Now **CLOSE** your handbook. **WRITE** the contractions of the following words. After you finish, go back to page 301 to check your work.

1. you are _____   4. they are _____

2. do not _____   5. is not _____

3. it is _____   6. was not _____

The poem is called "True Blue." .... *Using Punctuation*

TURN to page 302 in your handbook. Review the section "To Punctuate Titles." Now **TURN** to the chapter "Writing Free-Verse Poetry," which begins on page 177. On the lines below, **WRITE** the names of the model poems in this chapter. Use quotation marks correctly.

1. _____

2. _____

3. _____

The Name Game . . . . *Checking Mechanics*

OPEN your handbook to page 309, "Capitalizing Geographic Names." For each type of name listed (Planets and heavenly bodies, Continents, and so on), **LIST** another example. Do as many as you can on your own. **CHECK** a map or an atlas if you need help.

Words or numerals? . . . . *Checking Mechanics*

STUDY page 311 in your handbook. Then **FILL IN** the blanks in the following sentences. **WRITE** either "words" or "numerals," whichever is correct. Look back at page 311 to check your work.

1. When numbers begin a sentence, they are always written as _____.

2. Numbers less than 10 are almost always written as _____.

3. Numbers greater than 10 are almost always written as _____.

4. When you write very large numbers, you can use a combination of

   _____ and _____.

5. Numbers that are in dates, times, and addresses are written as _____.

6. Numbers that are amounts of money are written as _____.

Mail from AL to WY .... *Checking Mechanics*

OPEN your handbook to page 313. On the chart of state abbreviations,
LOOK UP the postal abbreviations for the following places. The first
one has been done for you.

Texas _____TX_____

District of Columbia _____

New York _____

Michigan _____

Florida _____

California _____

Utah _____

West Virginia _____

Kansas _____

Connecticut _____

Indiana _____

Mississippi _____

What does that spell? .... *Checking Mechanics*

TURN to page 312 in your handbook. Study the section "Acronyms."
Then **WRITE** the acronyms for the following phrases.

Rainforest Action Network _____

Performing Animal Welfare Society _____

Handicapped Equestrian Learning Program _____

North Atlantic Treaty Organization _____

Cooperative (for) American Relief Everywhere _____

Mothers Against Drunk Driving _____

National Aeronautics (and) Space Administration _____

It's time to give the turtle its food. .... *Using the Right Word*

It's is a pronoun. (Remember: A pronoun is a word that takes the place of a noun.) ***It's*** is a contraction that stands for ***it is***. **WRITE** two sentences. In one sentence, use ***its*** correctly. In your other sentence, use ***it's*** correctly. If you need help, see page 320 in your handbook. Or just **CHECK OUT** the title of this minilesson!

Their portfolios are over there. .... *Using the Right Word*

Their is a pronoun. It takes the place of a noun. ***There*** is an adverb that tells ***where***. **WRITE** two sentences. In one sentence, use ***their*** correctly. In your other sentence, use ***there*** correctly. If you need help, see page 322 in your handbook. Or just **CHECK OUT** the title of this minilesson.

"I won another one!" .... *Using the Right Word*

FILL IN the blanks in the sentences below using ***one*** or ***won*** correctly. **CHECK** page 321 in your handbook for help.

1. I _____ two hamsters at the picnic.

2. My dad said I could only keep _____ .

3. "But, Dad!" I said. "I_____ them!"

4. "Sorry," he said. "You have to give _____ away."

5. So I gave _____ to my friend Samantha.

6. Samantha's mom told me, "Stacy, I wish you had _____ two cakes instead of two hamsters!"

130 *Minilessons*

What do you know? . . . . *Understanding Sentences*

WRITE sentence fragments that give facts about people in your class. Write two fragments that need a verb. (*EXAMPLE:* Last summer, Kirsten.) Write two fragments that need a subject. (*EXAMPLE:* Has a pet snake.) **TRADE** with a partner. Try to turn each other's fragments into correct, complete sentences.

Put a stop to run-ons! . . . . *Understanding Sentences*

CHOOSE a paragraph from one of your favorite books or stories. **TURN** some of the sentences into run-on sentences. (See page 71 in your handbook for an explanation.) **TRADE** with a partner. **CORRECT** each other's run-ons by turning each one into two correct sentences. Finally, **COMPARE** your corrected sentences with the sentences in the book or story. (They don't have to be the same, but they do have to be correct.)

My Favorite Movie . . . . *Understanding Sentences*

TURN the following sentence fragment into a complete sentence:

My favorite movie.

EXAMPLE: My favorite movie is <u>Pocahontas</u>.

Now **TURN** your complete sentence into a run-on sentence by adding another complete thought to it.

EXAMPLE: My favorite movie is <u>Pocahontas</u> I really like the music.

Finally, **CORRECT** your run-on sentence.

EXAMPLE: My favorite movie is <u>Pocahontas</u>. I really like the music.

Which is it? . . . . *Understanding Sentences*

GET OUT an old story or report you have written. **PICK OUT** all of the simple and compound sentences. (See page 327 in your handbook to review simple and compound sentences.) **WRITE** an S at the beginning of each simple sentence. **WRITE** a C at the beginning of each compound sentence.

Be a sentence detective. . . . . . . *Understanding Sentences*

TURN to page 251 in your handbook. **READ** the student model "Skunks." **FIND** one example of each kind of sentence— declarative, interrogative, imperative, and exclamatory—in this writing. (Page 327 in your handbook explains the different kinds of sentences.) This is a good activity to do with a partner.

Finding Subjects and Predicates . . . . *Understanding Sentences*

CHOOSE an old story or report you have written. In each of your sentences, draw one line under the simple subject and two lines under the simple predicate. (See handbook pages 325-326.) Things to remember:

1. Compound sentences will have two subjects and two predicates.
2. Some simple sentences may have a compound subject or a compound verb.

Calling All Nouns . . . . *Understanding Our Language*

PRACTICE finding nouns. (Remember, a noun names a person, a place, a thing, or an idea.) First **TURN** to page 88 in your handbook. **FIND** all the nouns in the paragraph "Short and Quick." **LIST** the nouns below. (*Hint: Someone* is a pronoun, not a noun. There are eight nouns in all.)

1. _____   5. _____

2. _____   6. _____

3. _____   7. _____

4. _____   8. _____

Whose hair? . . . . *Understanding Our Language*

TURN to page 330 in your handbook. **READ** about "Possessive Pronouns." Then **USE** each of the following possessive pronouns in a sentence. Make all your sentences about hair. The first one has been done for you.

1. **their:** _Tracey and Maria wear their hair the same way._

2. **your:** _____

3. **my:** _____

4. **our:** _____

What a joke! . . . . *Understanding Our Language*

TURN to page 330 in your handbook. **READ** about "Common Personal Pronouns." Now turn to page 90. Read the friendly note under "To Share Something You Know." **LIST** all the personal pronouns you find in this note. There are six of them.

We flew in a helicopter. . . . . . *Understanding Our Language*

OPEN your handbook to page 331. **REVIEW** "Types of Verbs." Now **WRITE** three sentences about something your whole class did together. It could be a project or a field trip. In your first sentence, use an action verb. In your second sentence, use a linking verb. In your third sentence, use a helping verb.

It will snow tomorrow. . . . . . *Understanding Our Language*

TURN to page 56 in your handbook. Read the model "Snow Day!" All the verbs in this paragraph are in the past tense. Now **PRETEND** that you can predict the future. As you read the model aloud, **CHANGE** all the verbs to future tense. (*Hint:* You'll use the word *will* in every sentence.) We've written the first sentence below to get you started.

It will snow a lot tomorrow, so school will let out early.

Describe It .... *Understanding Our Language*

REVIEW "Adjectives" on page 335 in your handbook. Now turn to page 185. Read the haiku at the bottom of the page. It begins "See the red berries . . ." **FIND** the three adjectives in the haiku. Then **REPLACE** all three adjectives with new ones. Use any adjectives you want! See how your adjectives change the whole poem?

Quickly or slowly? .... *Understanding Our Language*

TURN to page 337 in your handbook. **REVIEW** "Adverbs." On a separate sheet of paper, **DRAW** a describing wheel. (If you need to see what a describing wheel looks like, turn to page 265.) The subject of your describing wheel is *run*. **ADD** as many adverbs as you can think of. *Remember:* Adverbs can tell *how* something is done, *where* it is done, or *when* it is done.

Prepositions in a Poem ..... *Understanding Our Language*

TURN to page 338 in your handbook. **READ** about "Prepositions." Now **TURN** to page 180. Look at the poem "When I Grow Up." **FIND** the prepositional phrases in this poem. (There are five of them.) **WRITE** the phrases on your own paper and **CIRCLE** the preposition in each one.

The Student Almanac

Say it with your hands. . . . . *Useful Tables and Lists*

LOOK at the sign language chart on page 343 in your handbook.
MEMORIZE the signs for the letters in your first name. **PRACTICE**
them until you can sign your name quickly.

Greetings! . . . . *Useful Tables and Lists*

TURN to page 344 in your handbook. **USE** the table to help you answer
the following questions. The first one has been done for you.

1. If you met a **Chinese** person,
   how would you say **hello**? _____ *dzău* _____

2. If you met a **French** person,
   how would you say **hello**? _____

3. How would you say **hello** to
   someone who speaks **Farsi**? _____

4. How would you say **hello** to
   someone who speaks **Spanish**? _____

5. How would you say **good-bye** to
   someone who speaks **Spanish**? _____

6. How would you say **good-bye** to
   someone who speaks **Swedish**? _____

7. What language uses the same
   word for **hello** and **good-bye**? _____

The bunny took a ride on the calf. . . . . *Useful Tables and Lists*

LOOK at the table of animal facts on page 345 in your handbook. **IMAGINE** that all of the *young* animals listed on this page went to summer camp together. **WRITE** a paragraph describing what some of the animals did at camp. Use the correct words for the young of at least four different animals.

The Geese and Swans of Puddle Lake . . . . *Useful Tables and Lists*

TURN to the table of animal facts on page 345 in your handbook. **IMAGINE** that you are studying ducks, geese, and swans. On a separate sheet of paper, **LIST** all the different words you could use for these three birds.

Cups, Pints, Quarts . . . . *Useful Tables and Lists*

TURN to page 346 in your handbook. **USE** the list of measurements to help you fill in the blanks below. (Look at the part of the list that gives **capacity** measures.) The first one has been done for you.

2 cups of orange juice   =   ___1___ **pint** of orange juice

4 cups of iced tea   =   _____ **pints** of iced tea

4 cups of iced tea   =   _____ **quart** of iced tea

16 cups of milk   =   _____ **pints** of milk

16 cups of milk   =   _____ **quarts** of milk

What does "mm" stand for? . . . . *Useful Tables and Lists*

OPEN your handbook to page 347. **USE** the list of metric measures to
help you fill in the blanks below. (Look under the heading **Length**.)
The first one has been done for you.

The letters **mm** stand for _____ millimeter _____ .

The letters **cm** stand for _____ .

The letter **m** stands for _____ .

The letters **km** stand for _____ .

One **kilometer** equals 1,000 _____ .

Space Travelers . . . . *Useful Tables and Lists*

DO this minilesson with a partner. Both of you **OPEN** your handbooks
to pages 348-349. You're going to take turns asking each other
questions about the table. **WRITE DOWN** two or three questions for
your partner to answer. *Remember:* You must ask questions that can
be answered by looking at the table. Below are two sample questions
you could ask.

1. Which planet is closest to the sun? _____ Mercury _____

2. Which planet has the most satellites? _____ Saturn _____

Watch me! . . . . *Improving Handwriting*

SELECT one letter in the alphabet. **REFER** to page 378 in the handbook to see how the letter is formed in cursive. **PRACTICE** writing this letter at the beginning, in the middle, and at the end of words. (Make sure you know both the lowercase and uppercase forms.) On the board, **SHOW** your classmates how to form this letter in different positions in words.

Bees buzz backward. . . . . *Improving Handwriting*

CREATE a tongue twister using as many *b* words as you can. **MAKE** a copy of your twister using your best cursive handwriting. **SHARE** your work with a classmate.

Note to Teachers: Create minilessons for other cursive letters posing special problems.

Speedy Delivery! . . . . *Improving Handwriting*

WRITE a friendly or funny note in cursive to a classmate. **DROP** it in his or her student mailbox, or **DELIVER** it in person. (Make sure to ask for a note in return.)

Final Check . . . . *Improving Handwriting*

WRITE the final copy of your next writing assignment in cursive. **EVALUATE** the quality of your handwriting using the checklist on page 379 in your handbook as a guide. (If you're not happy with your work, try again.)

Traveling Through History . . . . History in the Making

OPEN your handbook to the historical time line (pages 382-391). On the lines below, **WRITE** down who invented the steamboat, the bicycle, the gas-powered car, and the airplane. Also identify when each was invented. The first one has been done for you.

1. steamboat   _Robert Fulton_   _1802_

2. bicycle   _____   _____

3. car   _____   _____

4. airplane   _____   _____

The Start of Something Good . . . . History in the Making

Below are two lists: a list of foods and a list of dates. **DRAW** a line from the food to the date when you think it was invented. **FIND** each date on the time line in the handbook (pages 382-391) to check your work. How many did you get right?

popcorn	1630
hot dogs	1786
potato chips	1866
ice cream	1900
root beer	1925

Handbook

MINILESSONS

Answer Key

Provided in this section is an answer key for the few minilessons requiring specific answers. In most cases, the students' answers for the minilessons will vary.

The Process of Writing

Follow the Dotted Line . . . . *One Writer's Process*

Prewriting
Writing the First Draft
Revising
Editing and Proofreading
Publishing

Made by Peter . . . . *One Writer's Process*

(Answers may vary.)

1. During prewriting, Peter _picked a subject and collected details_.

2. When Peter wrote his first draft, he _put all of his ideas on_
   paper.

3. When Peter revised his draft, he _read his draft and changed_
   different parts.

4. During editing and proofreading, Peter _made sure his sentences_
   made sense, and he checked for errors.

5. When Peter published his story, he _shared it with his friends_.

Show me! . . . . One Writer's Process

(Answers will vary.)

1. My neighbor is old.

   My neighbor has white hair and a wrinkled face.

2. We were happy.

   We wore great big grins.

3. We were sad.

   We cried so much it hurt.

4. Our classroom is interesting.

   Our class belongs in Ripley's Believe It or Not.

Topic Sentence . . . . Writing Paragraphs

	subject	focus
p. 58, "Cooking with Grandma"	grandma & I	cooked in
		the backyard
p. 59, "Zev's Deli"	Zev's Deli	is one of my
		favorite places to go
p. 60, "Living with a Little Brother"	Living with a	can be hard
	little brother	
p. 61, "No Way to Go!"	Our neighborhood	needs sidewalks

Types of Paragraphs ....Writing Paragraphs

__b__ 1. expository   a. tells a story

__a__ 2. narrative   b. explains something

__d__ 3. descriptive   c. tries to get readers to agree

__c__ 4. persuasive   d. describes a person, place, or thing

People Watching ....Combining Sentences

1. Sam likes pineapple pizza. Dave likes pineapple pizza.

   Sam and Dave like pineapple pizza.

2. They made their own pizza. They made it yesterday.

   They made their own pizza yesterday.

3. Sam spread the dough. Sam poured on the sauce.

   Sam spread the dough and poured on the sauce.

4. Dave chopped the pineapple. Dave sprinkled it on the pizza.

   Dave chopped the pineapple and sprinkled it on the pizza.

The Forms of Writing

Five-Part Harmony . . . . *Writing Friendly Letters*

heading
salutation
body
closing
signature

Knowing Your A's and B's . . . . *Writing Alphabet Books*

(Answers will vary.)

A ustralia is a huge island known for its kangaroos .

B elgium .

C anada .

D omincan Republic .

E gypt .

The Words of Books . . . . *Writing Book Reviews*

1. Dialogue   is the talking between characters.

2. Fiction   is an invented or made-up story.

3. The plot   is the action in a story.

4. The setting   is the time and place of a story.

And the Envelope, Please .... *Writing Business Letters*

THE PRESIDENT OF THE UNITED STATES
THE WHITE HOUSE
1600 PENNSYLVANIA AVE
WASHINGTON DC 20500

The Tools of Learning

Just the Right Word .... *Building Vocabulary Skills*

Possible synonyms: sprint, jog, dash, bound, gallop, trot

First Cousins .... *Becoming a Better Speller*

Possible word relations: rainbow
raincoat
raindrop
rainfall
rainstorm
rainy
rained

The Proofreader's Guide

Don't forget contractions! . . . . *Using Punctuation*

1. you are ___you're___
2. do not ___don't___
3. it is ___it's___
4. they are ___they're___
5. is not ___isn't___
6. was not ___wasn't___

The poem is called "True Blue." . . . . *Using Punctuation*

1. ___"Elephant Poem"___
2. ___"No Homework"___
3. ___"When I Grow Up"___

Words or numerals? . . . . *Checking Mechanics*

1. When numbers begin a sentence,
   they are always written as _____words_____.

2. Numbers less than 10 are
   almost always written as _____words_____.

3. Numbers greater than 10 are
   almost always written as _____numerals_____.

4. When you write very large numbers, you can use a combination of

   _____numerals_____ and _____words_____.

5. Numbers that are in dates, times,
   and addresses are written as _____numerals_____.

6. Numbers that are amounts
   of money are written as _____numerals_____.

Mail from GA to WY . . . . *Checking Mechanics*

Texas	TX	District of Columbia	DC
New York	NY	Michigan	MI
Florida	FL	California	CA
Utah	UT	West Virginia	WV
Kansas	KS	Connecticut	CT
Indiana	IN	Mississippi	MS

What does that spell? . . . . *Checking Mechanics*

Rainforest Action Network _____RAN_____

Performing Animal Welfare Society _____PAWS_____

Handicapped Equestrian Learning Program _____HELP_____

North Atlantic Treaty Organization _____NATO_____

Cooperative (for) American Relief Everywhere _____CARE_____

Mothers Against Drunk Driving _____MADD_____

National Aeronautics (and) Space Administration _____NASA_____

"I won another one!" . . . . *Using the Right Word*

1. I _____won_____ two hamsters at the picnic.

2. My dad said I could only keep _____one_____ .

3. "But, Dad!" I said. "I_____won_____ them!"

4. "Sorry," he said. "You have to give _____one_____ away."

5. So I gave _____one_____ to my friend Samantha.

6. Samantha's mom told me, "Stacy, I wish you had _____won_____ two cakes instead of two hamsters!"

Calling All Nouns .... *Understanding Our Language*

1. notes
2. letters
3. envelope
4. stamp
5. note
6. person
7. fun
8. note

What a joke! .... *Understanding Our Language*

you, my, it, it, it, you

It will snow tomorrow. ...... *Understanding Our Language*

It will snow a lot tomorrow, so school will let out early. It will start to snow before lunch. At first, a few big flakes will come floating down. But then it will come down harder and harder. Snow will pile up on the playground. At 12:30, the principal will announce that school will let out at 1:00. Thanks to the snowstorm, we will have a free afternoon!

Quickly or slowly? . . . . *Understanding Our Language*

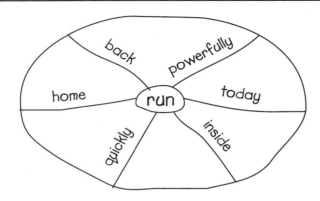

Prepositions in a Poem . . . . . *Understanding Our Language*

(of) cats

(on) her toes

(of) daisies and roses

(for) kids

(like) me

The Student Almanac

Greetings! . . . . *Useful Tables and Lists*

1. If you met a **Chinese** person, how would you say **hello**? ___ dzău ___

2. If you met a **French** person, how would you say **hello**? ___ bonjour ___

3. How would you say **hello** to someone who speaks **Farsi**? ___ salaam ___

4. How would you say **hello** to someone who speaks **Spanish**? ___ holá ___

5. How would you say **good-bye** to someone who speaks **Spanish**? ___ adiós ___

6. How would you say **good-bye** to someone who speaks **Swedish**? ___ adjö ___

7. What language uses the same word for **hello** and **good-bye**? ___ Hebrew ___

The Geese and Swans of Puddle Lake . . . . *Useful Tables and Lists*

duck: drake, duckling, brace/herd
goose: gander, gosling, flock/gaggle
swan: cob, pen, cygnet, bevy/flock

Cups, Pints, Quarts . . . . *Useful Tables and Lists*

2 cups of orange juice   =   __1__   **pint** of orange juice

4 cups of iced tea   =   __2__   **pints** of iced tea

4 cups of iced tea   =   __1__   **quart** of iced tea

16 cups of milk   =   __8__   **pints** of milk

16 cups of milk   =   __4__   **quarts** of milk

What does "mm" stand for? . . . . *Useful Tables and Lists*

The letters **mm** stand for __millimeter__ .

The letters **cm** stand for __centimeter__ .

The letter **m** stands for __meter__ .

The letters **km** stand for __kilometer__ .

One **kilometer** equals 1,000 __meters__ .

Traveling Through History . . . . *History in the Making*

1.	steamboat	Robert Fulton	1802
2.	bicycle	Kirkpatrick Macmillan	1839
3.	car	Charles and Frank Duryea	1893
4.	airplane	Orville and Wilbur Wright	1903

The Start of Something Good

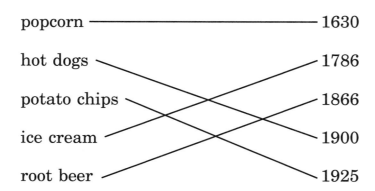

popcorn ———————————— 1630

hot dogs 1786

potato chips 1866

ice cream 1900

root beer 1925

Evaluating/Assessing

MONITORING

The information in this section will help you evaluate your students' language and learning progress. Included are some general evaluating guidelines; specific strategies for evaluating basic skills, handwriting, and writing; and evaluating and responding masters that you can use with your students.

Evaluating Your Students' Work

The ultimate goal of evaluation should be to help students improve their overall language proficiency. The guidelines and strategies that follow have been designed with these important points in mind.

Special Note: To help students become active participants in the evaluation process, make sure that they know how to use *Write on Track*. It's especially important that they become familiar with "The Process of Writing" section.

How should I evaluate my students?

The best methods of evaluation are those that address the process of learning as much (or more) than the end products of learning. Evaluation should be . . .

— based on a learner's overall performance,
— interesting and functional in design,
— open-ended and flexible in scope, and
— meaningful and relevant to the learner.

In other words, the evaluation of students should be as *authentic* as possible.

What is meant by authentic assessment?

Authentic assessment is based on the principle that evaluation informs instruction. Authentic assessment is carried out through observations, interactions, and analysis.

— When you *observe* a student at work, make note of his or her enthusiasm, diligence, care, creativity, neatness, and so on.
— When you *interact* with a student, informally question him or her about the work in progress. Also engage in small-group discussions and conduct student/teacher conferences.
— When you *analyze* a student's work, carefully examine his or her finished product. Highlight particular strengths; make suggestions for upcoming assignments; note your overall impressions; and award a point total, mark, or comment.

Should I employ all three of these methods of evaluation each time my students work on an activity?

No, it would be next to impossible to observe and interact with students as well as analyze their work for each and every activity. However, we do encourage you to make use of all three methods of assessment throughout the course of the school year.

How should I evaluate writing?

As you know, a great deal has been "written" about the teaching of writing, including how to evaluate writing as a process rather than an end product. We have encapsulated much of this information starting on page 163 in this section. Insights into assessing writing in progress (formative evaluation) as well as insights into assessing the end results of writing (summative evaluation) are addressed on these pages.

Recently, much attention has been given to special writing portfolios in which students showcase their best writing for evaluation at the end of a grading period. Portfolios place a significant part of the assessment process in the hands of the student writers because they can pick and choose what they want evaluated. Students appreciate the sense of ownership this gives them. Teachers appreciate portfolios because they reduce the number of finished papers they have to assess. (Guidelines for using writing portfolios are included in this section starting on page 167. There is also a section on portfolios in the *Write on Track* student handbook, pages 26-29.)

Note: Keep in mind that the type of writing done by the students determines the level of evaluation called for. Certain forms of personal or exploratory writing should be awarded a basic performance score plus a positive comment or two. A more complete writing project naturally demands more thorough analysis.

How should I address basic skills?

It has been demonstrated in study after study that learning the basic skills of grammar and punctuation out of context has little relevance for young learners and little carryover when they are involved in authentic language experiences. Students learn about their language when they put language to good use. That is, they learn about their language when they thoughtfully read, write, speak, listen, and think.

When you notice that a student has difficulty with a particular skill, help him or her deal with this problem. There's little incentive to learn if you penalize students for making particular errors in an individual piece of writing. There's all the incentive in the world to learn if you reward them for attempting to correct the error over the long term. Always remember that evaluation informs instruction.

Helping Each Student: Let's say one of your student writers doesn't always remember to put end punctuation marks after her or his sentences. You can do a number of things:

— First note the problem. Make it clear to the student what the problem is and why it is a problem.

— Then refer the student to the handbook to learn how to correct the problem.

— Also have the student keep track of this error in a special section of a notebook, so he or she will know what to look for in the next piece of writing.

Helping a Small Group: If you feel the problem is common to many students in the class, consider assigning a related minilesson, to address the problem. (See pages 99-156 in this guide for minilessons.)

Let students know that you expect them to watch for the problem in future writing assignments. Then, when you evaluate their work at the end of the term, check to see what progress they are making.

What about handwriting?

Always remember that handwriting is not an end in itself. Students *use* handwriting to express themselves on paper. The main point of evaluation should be to encourage and help students write more legibly and fluently over the long term. Students can evaluate their handwriting for final drafts using the handwriting checklist on page 379 in *Write on Track*.

Should I do all of the evaluating?

No, evaluation should be part of the learning process and should involve students as much as possible. Students automatically become involved in the process if they complete self-evaluation sheets or briefly reflect on their learning progress in a notebook or journal. Questions students might ask of themselves include the following: *Did things go as I planned in this activity? What did I like the best about my work? What caused me the most problems? What could I do to improve my work the next time we do this type of activity?*

Students can also participate in peer-evaluation conferences or peer-response groups. These conferences work best if students have a predetermined checklist or guide with which to judge their peers' work. (See pages 169-171 in this section for example conferencing sheets.)

Special Note: Don't expect students to be careful, insightful, and fair evaluators right from the start. This will come only through guided practice. (The *Write on Track* student handbook contains information on conferencing with partners.)

Parents should also be involved in the evaluation process. For example, they can be encouraged to react (via written messages or in conferences) to their child's work, whether it be a series of daily assignments or a more important piece of writing. They can also react to their child's portfolio at the end of a grading period.

Should I assign a grade or mark for each activity?

We certainly don't recommend it. You don't have the time to review each activity carefully enough to assign a grade. On top of that, grading each activity is not a productive method of evaluating. Grades generally get in the way of learning because they represent a stopping point, an end result. A more open-ended system of evaluation is much more in line with current thinking.

We believe that a basic "performance" score is sufficient for most of the activities. All you have to do is assign students a predetermined number of points (5), a comment (Excellent), or a mark (+) upon completion of their work. (The score they receive depends on their basic performance.) We also believe teachers should make at least one specific, positive comment on individual activities whenever possible.

How do I evaluate the students' work at the end of the quarter or semester?

If your students keep folders of their work and evaluations, you have a complete file for each student. You may also have students showcase their best work in a portfolio. If you noted observations and interactions during various activities, you have your own personal comments and reactions to consider. With these materials in place, you have more than enough information to assess each student's performance.

Make sure your criteria for grading reflect each student's progress as a language learner as much as (or more than) they reflect end products.

Evaluating Writing: A Closer Look

Two kinds of evaluation interest teachers today: **formative evaluation** (evaluating while the students are developing their writing) and **summative evaluation** (evaluating the outcome of the students' efforts). Formative evaluation does not result in a grade; summative evaluation usually does. Some teachers choose to give students a set number of points (a performance score) during different stages in the formative writing process.

Formative Evaluation

Formative evaluation is most often used for writing-to-learn activities, prewriting activities, writing in progress, journal entries, and so forth. Three types of formative evaluation at the elementary level are widely used: the individual conference, the small-group conference, and peer conferencing.

The Individual Conference

The individual conference can occur informally at the student's deskside, or it can take place at a scheduled time. In the early stages of the writing process, responses and questions should be about writing ideas, content, audience, purpose, generating ideas, and so on. Questions should be open-ended. This gives the writer "space" to talk. When a writer is talking, he or she is thinking, clarifying, and making decisions. Teachers don't have to attempt to solve problems for their students, but they can ask questions and suggest possible solutions.

In the editing and proofreading stage, a teacher might ask, "Why do you need a period here?" Students should try to answer the question and add the necessary punctuation marks. With the inexperienced writer, it's best not to mark all errors. Simply draw a double line to indicate where you stopped editing or proofreading the student's work. An individual conference can also be student directed if he or she finishes a draft, identifies a problem, or wants to share a breakthrough.

"Teachers need to look at each individual writer, and what's more, each writer will demonstrate different writing behaviors with different writing tasks."
—Jo-Ann Parry and David Hornsby
Write On: A Conference Approach to Writing

The Small-Group Conference

The small-group conference may consist of groups of three to five students who are at the same stage in the writing process or who are involved in the same type of writing project. The goals of a small-group conference are to help students improve their own writing and become writing evaluators for others. Minilessons work well in small-group conferences.

Consider holding a publisher's meeting during small-group conferences so students can help one another select writing to be published. Your role is to help students reach informed conclusions about their writing. For more about this type of evaluation, see "Publishing Your Writing" on pages 30-33 in *Write on Track*.

Peer Conferencing

Students need to learn how to conference with others (without the help of a teacher). We suggest that students work in pairs at first and use some type of checklist or guide when they conference. Always model how to use the checklist before you have students work on their own. Impose a time limit for peer-responding sessions to keep students on task (10-15 minutes).

To help your students prepare for peer-conferencing sessions, have them read "Conferencing with Partners" (pages 48-51) in *Write on Track*.

One very simple process to use for peer responding is to ask a student to read his or her partner's paper and then generate three questions beginning with *who, what, where, when, why,* or *how.* The questions and paper are returned to the writer, who then responds to these questions. These questions serve as a starting point for a discussion. Students could also use one of the conferencing sheets provided at the end of this section. (See pages 169-171.)

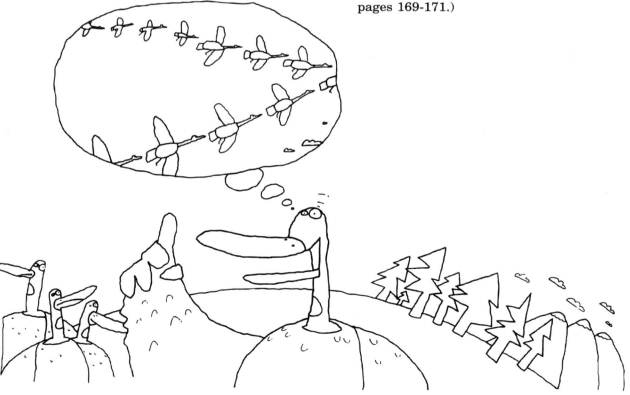

Summative Evaluation

We want students to value the writing process as much as, if not more than, the final product, and we want their attention to be on personal goals, not grades. However, the day will come when a grade must be assigned to at least some of their completed work. This is when summative evaluation is important. Here are some general principles to help you evaluate finished pieces.

1. Clearly establish the criteria for evaluating each piece of writing. Limit the criteria so you do not overwhelm the students or yourself.

2. Ask students to help you develop the criteria. This can be done in individual conferences or with the entire class. Students readily accept and understand criteria they have helped build.

3. Students must have ample opportunities for formative evaluation before their final products receive grades. And students deserve points for the work they have done during the writing process.

4. Concern for content, fluency, and fresh ideas should be given high priority during summative evaluation. Correctness and neatness are important, but they are only part of the complete writing picture.

5. Students should be involved in summative evaluation. You can do this by providing students with a form that asks them to identify the best parts of their writing, list the problems they encountered, draw a circle around the parts they would work on if they had more time, and so on. In addition to the above ideas, students should be asked how much time they put into a project and what grade they would assign to it.

Approaches for Summative Evaluating

Holistic grading evaluates a piece of writing as a whole. The most basic approach to holistic grading is to read the paper rather quickly for a general impression. The paper is graded according to this impression. A reader might also compare a particular piece with a number of pieces already graded, or rate it for the inclusion of features important to that type of writing.

Teachers can use a basic rubric like the one that follows to rate the effectiveness of a piece of writing.

WRITING RUBRIC

4 - Excellent The writing has a beginning, a middle, and an ending. The ideas are arranged in the best order. The writing contains interesting words and ideas. The writing is free of careless errors.

3 - Good The writing has a beginning, a middle, and an ending. Most of the ideas follow in order. A few details need to be added. The writing contains a few careless errors.

2 - Fair The writing doesn't have a clear beginning, middle, or ending. It needs reorganizing. Main ideas aren't well developed. The writing contains some careless errors.

1 - Weak The writing does not have a central focus and contains many errors.

Task-specific scoring accords a grade based on how well a student has accomplished specific rhetorical tasks. A teacher might, for example, create a scoring checklist or guide for a short fiction writing assignment. This checklist would include those elements that are inherent in this writing form—plot, characterization, point of view, and so on. Students must understand the criteria for scoring before they begin their writing. This type of grading addresses specific rather than open-ended writing assignments.

Portfolio grading gives students an opportunity to choose pieces of writing to be graded. This is a common method of evaluation in writing workshops where students keep all of their work in a writing folder. Teachers require them to submit a specified number of finished projects from their folder for grading each quarter or semester. Students enjoy this method of evaluation because it gives them some control over the evaluation process; teachers like it because it lessens their workload. They don't have to grade everything a student has written.

A **performance system** is a quick and simple method of evaluation. If students complete a writing activity, and it meets the previously established level of acceptability, they receive the preestablished grade or points for completing the assignment. The student either has or has not completed the activity.

Using Writing Portfolios

More and more, language arts teachers are making portfolios an important part of their writing programs. Will portfolios work for you? Will they help you and your students assess their writing? Read on and find out.

What is a classroom portfolio?

A writing portfolio is a limited collection of a student's writing for evaluation. It differs from the traditional writing folder that contains all of a student's work. A writing portfolio contains only a student's best efforts.

Why should I ask students to compile classroom portfolios?

Portfolios get students directly involved in the assessment process since they have to evaluate their own writing. Portfolios also make students accountable for their own writing progress. And they help students appreciate writing as an involved and recursive process of writing and rewriting.

You can employ any or all methods of assessment when portfolios are used, including self-evaluation, peer evaluation, contract writing, traditional grading, and so on.

How many pieces of writing should be included in a portfolio?

You and your students should really make that decision. You should, however, expect your students to compile at least three pieces of writing in a portfolio each quarter. (Some teachers have their students contract for a specific amount of required writing.) All drafts for each piece should be included. Generally, students are also required to include a reflective writing or self-critique sheet that assesses their writing progress.

Note: Some teachers want students to include in their portfolios one or two pieces of writing from other disciplines.

When do portfolios work best?

Students need plenty of class time to work on writing if they are going to produce effective portfolios. If they are used correctly, portfolios turn beginning writers into practicing writers. And practicing writers need regularly scheduled blocks of time to refine or work on their craft.

Portfolios are tailor-made for language arts classrooms that operate as writing workshops.

How can I help my students with their portfolio writing?

Give your students many opportunities to discuss their writing with their classmates. Make sharing sessions an important part of your class. Expect your students to evaluate their own writing and the writing of their peers—and help them to do so. Also provide students with guidance when they need help with their own writing. (Again, the handbook provides plenty of writing guidelines.) And create a stimulating classroom environment that encourages students to immerse themselves in writing.

How do I grade a portfolio?

Base each grade on goals you and your students establish at the beginning of the grading period and on what is achieved as evidenced in the portfolio. Many teachers develop a critique sheet for assessment that is based on the goals established by the class. (It's very important that students know how many pieces they should include in their portfolios, how their work should be arranged in their portfolios, how the portfolios will be assessed, and so on.)

Note: See pages 26-29 in the *Write on Track* handbook for student-directed material related to planning a portfolio. Also see pages 172-173 in this section of your guide for masters related to portfolios.

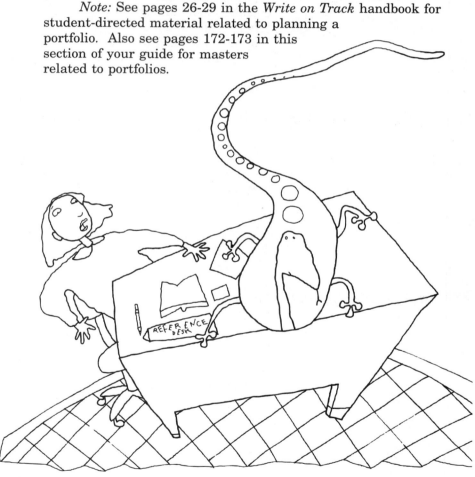

Memorable and More

DIRECTIONS: On the top half of this sheet, list the things you really like about a piece of writing. On the bottom half, list the suggestions or questions you may have.

Author _____ Title _____

Memorable

_____

_____

_____

_____

_____

More

_____

_____

_____

_____

_____

Conferencing Checklist

DIRECTIONS: Use this checklist when you are reacting to nonfiction writing. (Jot down questions and suggestions on the back of the conferencing sheet.)

Author _____ Title _____

Organization:

_____ Does the writing have a beginning, a middle, and an ending?

_____ Are all of the ideas in the best order?

Details:

_____ Do all of the details talk about the subject?

_____ Are there enough details and examples?

Style and Mechanics:

_____ Are the sentences easy to read?

Is the writing free of errors?

Tracking Your Writing

Conferencing
Sheet

Date _____

Title _____

1 **Read your draft to yourself.** ☐

2 **Read your draft two times to a friend.** ☐

3 **My friend's questions and suggestions:**

_____

_____

4 **Revise** (For example, add information if you need to.) ☐

5 **Edit your draft for**   Complete Sentences ☐

                        Best and Right Words ☐

6 **Proofread your draft for**   Spelling ☐

                        Punctuation and Capital Letters ☐

7 **Teacher Conference** _____ ☐
                                       Date

8 **Final Teacher Check** _____ ☐
                                       Date

Writing Reflections

I chose to put this piece of writing in my portfolio because _____

_____

_____

_____

_____

As I worked on this piece, I learned _____

_____

_____

_____

In my future writing, I would like to _____

_____

_____

_____

Portfolio Reflections

Dear _____,
We will meet soon to go over your portfolio. Before we do, I would like you to order your writing from the best piece to the piece that needs the most work. I will ask you the four questions below. Please think about each one before we meet on _____.

Thank you!

1. What makes this your best work? _____

_____

2. What are you able to do now as a writer that you couldn't do before? _____

_____

_____

3. What has helped you most with your writing this marking period? _____

_____

_____

4. What are your writing goals for the next period? _____

_____

Reading-Writing
CONNECTION

In this section, you will find lists of important, high-interest titles that relate to many chapters in *Write on Track*. These lists will prove invaluable when planning extended units for these chapters. Refer to the symbols for reading-level information. Titles without symbol labels have reading levels in the third-grade range.

Reading Levels: (E) = **Easy**
(C) = **Challenging**

Writing in Journals

Amelia's Notebook
by Marissa Moss, 1995

Arthur, for the Very First Time Ⓒ
by Patricia MacLachlan, 1980

Bluewater Journal Ⓒ
by Loretta Krupinski, 1995

Celia's Island Journal Ⓔ
by Celia Thaxter (Adapted by
Loretta Krupinski), 1992

Chasing After Annie
by Marjorie Weinman Sharmat, 1981

I Love Saturday Ⓔ
by Patricia Reilly Giff, 1991

Linnea's Almanac
by Christina Bjork, 1989

My Pet: A PhotoLog Book Ⓔ
by Janet Horowitz and
Kathy Faggela, 1992

Now Everybody Really Hates Me Ⓔ
by Jane Read Martin and
Patricia Marx, 1993

Only Opal: The Diary of a Young Girl
by Barbara Cooney, 1994

Scooter Ⓒ
by Vera B. Williams, 1993

Taxi Cat and Huey Ⓒ
by Gen LeRoy, 1992

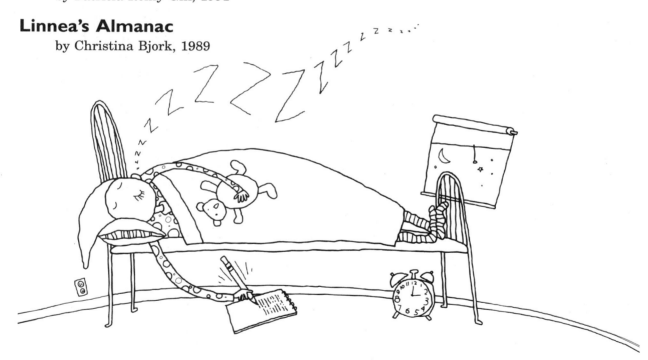

Reading Levels: Ⓔ = Easy
Ⓒ = Challenging

Making **Albums**

Carl Makes a Scrapbook (E)
by Alexendra Day, 1994

My Book About My Cat
by Sheldon Gertensfeld, V.M.D., 1994

My Book About My Dog
by Sheldon Gertensfeld, V.M.D., 1994

My Pet: A PhotoLog Book (E)
by Janet Horowitz and Kathy Faggela, 1992

Speak! Children's Book Illustrators Brag About Their Dogs (C)
Edited by Michael J. Rosen, 1993

Writing **Lists**

Frog and Toad Are Friends (E)
by Arnold Lobel, 1970

Moon Glows
by Berthea verDorn, 1990

One Gorilla (E)
by Atsuko Morozumi, 1990

The Tenth Good Thing About Barney (C)
by Judith Viorst

The Very Hungry Caterpillar (E)
by Eric Carle, 1969

Where the Sidewalk Ends (C)
by Shel Silverstein, 1974

Writing Friendly **Notes**

Arthur's Birthday (E)
by Marc Brown, 1989

How to Make Pop-Ups
by Joan Irvine, 1988

Writing Friendly **Letters**

Dear Annie
by Judith Caseley, 1991

Dear Brother (E)
by Frank Asch, 1992

The Jolly Christmas Postman (E)
by Janet Ahlberg and Allan Ahlberg, 1991

The Jolly Postman (E)
by Janet Ahlberg and Allan Ahlberg, 1986

Kate Heads West (E)
by Pat Brisson, 1990

A Letter to Amy (E)
by Ezra Jack Keats, 1968

Letters from Felix
by Annette Langen and
Constanza Droop, 1994

Mouse Letters
by Michelle Cartlidge, 1993

Your Best Friend, Kate (E)
by Pat Brisson, 1989

**Yours Affectionately,
Peter Rabbit**
by Beatrix Potter, 1984

Reading Levels: (E) = **Easy**
(C) = **Challenging**

Writing Personal Narratives

(Books that are written like personal narratives)

Alexander and the Terrible, Horrible, No Good, Very Bad Day
by Judith Viorst, 1987

Amy Elizabeth Explores Bloomingdale's Ⓔ
by E. L. Konigsburg, 1992

A Chair for My Mother
by Vera B. Williams, 1982

Fun/No Fun
by James Stevenson, 1994

Ira Says Goodbye
by Bernard Waber, 1988

July
by James Stevenson, 1990

Never Spit on Your Shoes Ⓔ
by Denys Cazet, 1990

The Rag Coat
by Lauren Mills, 1991

Smoky Nights
by Eve Bunting, 1994

Thunder Cake
by Patricia Polacco, 1990

The Wall
by Eve Bunting , 1990

Watch Out for the Chicken Feet in Your Soup
by Tomie dePaola, 1974

When I Was Young in the Mountains
by Cynthia Rylant, 1982

Writing Family **Stories**

Annie and the Old One (E)
by Miles Miska, 1971

A Birthday Basket for Tia (E)
by Pat Mora, 1992

The Canada Geese Quilt
by Natalie Kinsey-Warnock, 1989

A Forever Family
by Roslyn Banish, 1992

Go Fish
by Mary Stolz, 1991

Going West (E)
by Jean Van Leeuwen, 1992

The Hundred-Penny Box
by Sharon Bell Mathis, 1975

Miss Rumphius
by Barbara Cooney, 1982

The Moon Lady
by Amy Tan, 1992

"More, More, More," Said the Baby: Three Love Stories (E)
by Vera B. Williams, 1990

My Great-Aunt Arizona
by Gloria Houston, 1992

Shortcut (E)
by Donald Crews, 1992

Through Grandpa's Eyes
by Patricia MacLachlan, 1980

A Visit with Great-Grandma (E)
by Sharon Hart Addy, 1989

The Wednesday Surprise (E)
by Eve Bunting, 1989

Reading Levels: (E) = **Easy**
(C) = **Challenging**

Writing Alphabet Books

Aardvarks, Disembark! (E)
by Ann Jonas, 1990

The ABC's of Origami: Paper Folding for Children (C)
by Claude Sarasas, 1964

Alison's Zinnia (E)
by Anita Lobel, 1990

Alligator Arrived with Apples (E)
by Crescent Dragonwagon, 1987

Alphabestiary
by Jane Yolen, 1995

Alpha Beta Chowder
by Jeanne Steig, 1992

Alphabet Puzzle
by Jill Downie, 1988

Ashanti to Zulu: African Traditions
by Margaret Musgrove, 1976

Away from Home (E)
by Anita Lobel, 1994

Built in the USA: American Buildings from Airports to Zoos
Edited by Diane Maddix, 1985

City Seen from A to Z (E)
by Rachel Isadora, 1992

Jeremy Kooloo (E)
by Tim Mahurin, 1995

Let's Fly from A to Z (E)
by Doug Magee and
Robert Newman, 1992

The Little Cats ABC Book (E)
by Martin Leman, 1993

Once Upon A to Z: An Alphabet Oddysey
by Jody Linscott, 1991

Pedro, His Perro, and the Alphabet Sombrero
by Lynn Rowe, 1995

Potluck (E)
by Anne Shelby, 1991

Sharon, Lois & Bram Sing A to Z
by Sharon Hampson, et al, 1992

The Z Was Zapped: A Play in Twenty-Six Acts
by Chris Van Allsburg, 1987

Writing Newspaper Stories

Extra! Extra!: The Who, What, Where, When and Why of Newspapers Ⓒ
by Linda Garfield, 1993

The Furry News: How to Make a Newspaper
by Loreen Leedy, 1990

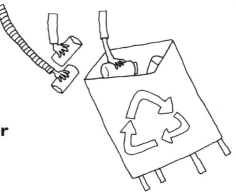

Writing to Explain

Acorn Pancakes, Dandelion Salad and 38 Other Recipes Ⓒ
by Jean Craighead George, 1995

Creepy Cuisine
by Lucy Monroe, 1993

Everybody Cooks Rice
by Norah Dooley, 1991

Hopscotch Around the World
by Mary Lankford, 1992

Roald Dahl's Revolting Recipes
by Roald Dahl, 1994

Sewing by Hand
by Christine Hoffman, 1994

**Syd Hoff's How to
Draw Dinosaurs** Ⓔ
by Syd Hoff, 1981

Using the Library

Find It! The Inside Story of Your Library Ⓒ
by Claire McInerney, 1989

Reading Levels: Ⓔ **= Easy**
Ⓒ **= Challenging**

Writing Classroom **Reports**

Big Cats
by Seymour Simon, 1991

Dinosaur Is the Biggest Animal That Ever Lived and Other Wrong Ideas You Thought Were True
by Seymour Simon, 1984

Discovery of the Americas
by Betsy & Giulio Maestro, 1990

If You Grew Up with Abraham Lincoln
by Ann McGovern, 1966

If You Grew Up with George Washington
by Ruth Belov Gross, 1982

Moon of the Bears Ⓒ
by Jean Craighead George, 1993

Moon of the Monarch Butterflies Ⓒ
by Jean Craighead George, 1993

One Day in the Tropical Rainforest Ⓒ
by Jean Craighead George, 1990

The Puffins Are Back
by Gail Gibbons, 1991

Rock
by Peter Parnall, 1991

Sharks Ⓔ
by Gail Gibbons, 1992

Snakes
by Seymour Simon, 1992

Volcanoes Ⓒ
by Seymour Simon, 1988

Whales Ⓔ
by Gail Gibbons, 1991

Windows for Kids
by William Sanders, 1992

Woodpile
by Peter Parnall, 1990

Writing Photo Essays

Brothers and Sisters
> by Maxine Rosenberg (Photos by George Ancona), 1991

Come Back, Salmon: How a Group of Dedicated Kids Adopted Pigeon Creek and Brought It Back to Life
> Photos by Sidnee Wheelwright, 1992

Families: A Celebration of Diversity, Commitment, and Love
> by Aylette Jenness, 1990

Handtalk School
> by Mary Beth Miller and George Ancona (Photos by George Ancona), 1991

I Love Guinea Pigs
> by Dick King-Smith, 1995

Light and Shadow
> by Myra Cohn Livingston (Photos by Barbara Rogasky), 1992

Michael Chang: Tennis Champion Ⓔ
> by Pamela Dell, 1995

Rosie, a Visiting Dog's Story
> by Stephanie Calmenson, 1994

Searching for Laura Ingalls: A Reader's Journey Ⓒ
> by Kathryn Lasky and Meribah Knight (Photos by Christopher G. Knight), 1993

A Very Young Musician
> by Jill Krementz, 1991

Voices from the Fields: Children of Migrant Farm Workers Tell Their Stories Ⓒ
> by S. Beth Atkin, 1993

Reading Levels: Ⓔ = Easy
Ⓒ = Challenging

Writing Realistic **Stories**

Writing Time-Travel Fantasies

Cat and Alex and the Magic Flying Carpet (E)
by Robin Ballard, 1991

The Christmas Ark
by Robert D. San Souci, 1991

Earth Words (C)
by Seymour Simon, 1995

Everyone Knows What a Dragon Looks Like (E)
by Jay Williams, 1976

Fat Men from Space
by Daniel Pinkwater, 1977

Matthew Looney (C)
by Jerome Beatty, 1972

Medallion of the Black Hound (C)
by S. R. Murphy, 1989

My Robot Buddy
by A. Slote, 1986

My Trip to Alpha I
by A. Slote, 1992

Omega Station
by A. Slote, 1986

An Ordinary Cat (E)
by Christine Kettner, 1991

Time Train (E)
by Paul Fleischman, 1994

Wilbur's Space Machine (E)
by Lorna Balian, 1990

Reading Levels: (E) = **Easy**
(C) = **Challenging**

Writing **Plays**

Aesop in the Afternoon
by Albert Cullum, 1972

East of the Sun and West of the Moon: A Play
by Nancy Willard, 1989

Funny Skits and Sketches
by Terry Halligan, 1987

Goldilocks and the Three Bears Ⓔ
by Tony Ross, 1992

Just a Minute
by Irene N. Watts, 1990

The Stinky Cheese Man: And Other Fairly Stupid Tales
by Jon Scieszka, 1992

The True Story of the Three Little Pigs Ⓔ
by Jon Scieszka, 1989

Writing Free-Verse **Poetry**

And the Green Grass Grew All Around
Collected by Alvin Schwartz, 1992

Creatures of Earth, Sea, and Sky
by Georgia Heard, 1992

Demi's Secret Garden Ⓔ
Compiled by Demi, 1993

Follow the Moon
by Sarah Weeks, 1995

Hand in Hand: An American History Through Poetry
Edited by Lee Bennett Hopkins, 1994

Night on Neighborhood Street
by Eloise Greenfield, 1991

Remembering and Other Poems
by Myra Cohn Livingston, 1989

Sing to the Sun
by Ashley Bryan, 1992

Where Fish Go in Winter and Answers to Other Great Mysteries Ⓔ
by Amy G. Koss, 1987

Where the Sidewalk Ends Ⓒ
by Shel Silverstein, 1974

Writing Other Forms of **Poetry**

The Completed Hickory Dickory Dock Ⓔ
by Jim Aylesworth, 1990

Dinosaur Dances Ⓒ
by Jane Yolen, 1990

Haiku Is . . . a Feeling
by Edith M. Leivis, 1990

**In the Eyes of the Cat: Japanese Poetry for
All Seasons** Ⓒ
Compiled by Demi, 1992

In a Spring Garden Ⓔ
Selected by Richard Lewis, 1965

Lots of Limericks
by Myra Cohn Livingston, 1991

Miss Mary Mack and Other Children's Street Rhymes
by Joanna Cole and Stephanie Calmenson, 1990

My Song Is Beautiful—Poems and Pictures in Many Voices
Selected by Mary Ann Hoberman, 1994

One Sun: A Book of Terse Verse Ⓔ
by Bruce McMillan, 1990

Ride a Purple Pelican Ⓔ
by Jack Prelutsky, 1986

Reading Levels: Ⓔ **= Easy**
Ⓒ **= Challenging**

BIBLIOGRAPHY

The "references" in the bibliography list titles that were consulted during the development of each handbook chapter and coordinating program activities. The "resources" list important titles teachers may consult for additional information related to each chapter.

Bibliography

THE PROCESS OF WRITING

Getting Started

REFERENCES

All About Writing
Calkins, Lucy McCormick. *Living Between the Lines*. Portsmouth: Heinemann, 1991.

One Writer's Process
Millett, Nancy C. *Teaching the Writing Process*. Boston: Houghton Mifflin Company, 1986.

Writing with a Computer
Collins, James L., and Elizabeth A. Sommers. *Writing On-Line*. Portsmouth: Heinemann, 1985.

Planning Portfolios
Rief, Linda. "Finding the Value in Portfolios." *Seeking Diversity*. Portsmouth: Heinemann, 1992.

Publishing Your Writing
Tompkins, Gail E. *Teaching Writing*. New York: Macmillan College Publishing Company, 1993.

RESOURCES

Golub, Jeffrey N. "Computers in English Instruction." *Activities for an Interactive Classroom*. Urbana: National Council of Teachers of English, 1994. (Includes a chapter on using the word processor for revision.)

Graves, Donald. *Writing: Teachers and Children at Work*. Portsmouth: Heinemann, 1983. (Shows teachers and students writing, conferencing, and learning together. This book has become the classic text in the movement to make writing a central part of the classroom.)

Graves, Donald, and Bonnie S. Sunstein. *Portfolio Portraits*. Portsmouth: Heinemann, 1992. (Contains unique portraits of portfolio keepers.)

Murray, Donald M. *Learning by Teaching*. Portsmouth: Boynton Cook, 1982. (Offers insights into the process of writing and the process of teaching.)

Prewriting and Drafting Guide

REFERENCES

Building a File of Writing Ideas

Asher, Sandy. *Where Do You Get Your Ideas?* New York: Walker and Company, 1987.

Kovacs, Deborah, and James Prowler. *Meet the Authors and Illustrators: 60 Creators of Favorite Children's Books Talk About Their Work.* New York: Scholastic, 1991.

Collecting Details

Graves, Donald. *Investigate Nonfiction.* Portsmouth: Heinemann, 1989.

Planning and Drafting Guide

Jett-Simpson, Mary, and Lauren Leslie. "Writing Development." *Ecological Assessment.* Schofield (WI): Wisconsin State Reading Association, 1994.

RESOURCES

Fletcher, Ralph. *What a Writer Needs.* Portsmouth: Heinemann, 1993. (Contains short essays on the writer's craft, from the art of using details to developing voice.)

Gail, Donald R., ed. *Speaking for Ourselves: Autobiographical Sketches by Notable Authors of Books for Young Adults.* Urbana: National Council of Teachers of English, 1990. (Presents insights into the writing habits of popular authors.)

Gould, June. "Rehearsal: Hauling the Line" and "Prewriting: Building a Universe." *The Writer in All of Us.* New York: Dayton, 1989. (Geared for older writers, but offers many practical prewriting ideas.)

Rico, Gabriel L. *Writing the Natural Way: Using Right-Brain Techniques to Release Your Expressive Powers.* Los Angeles: Tarcher, 1983. (See, especially, chapter 2, "Clustering: Doorway to Your Design Mind.")

Revising, Conferencing, and Editing Guide

REFERENCES

Revising Your Writing

Fletcher, Ralph. *What a Writer Needs*. Portsmouth: Heinemann, 1993.

Murray, Donald M. *Learning by Teaching*. Upper Montclair: Boynton Cook, 1982.

Conferencing with Partners

Calkins, Lucy McCormick. *The Art of Teaching Writing*. New edition. Portsmouth: Heinemann, 1994.

Nathan, Ruth, et al. *Classroom Strategies That Work: An Elementary Teacher's Guide to Process Writing*. Portsmouth: Heinemann, 1989.

Editing and Proofreading

Sebranek, Patrick, Verne Meyer, and Dave Kemper. *Write Source 2000: A Guide to Writing, Thinking, and Learning*. Lexington (MA): D.C. Heath, 1995.

RESOURCES

Asher, Sandy. *Wild Words! How to Train Them to Tell Stories*. New York: Walker and Company, 1989. (Written for children, this book will help all writers revise their fiction. The author goes into great detail about showing rather than telling.)

Robb, Laura. *Whole Language, Whole Learners: Creating a Literature-Centered Classroom*. New York: William Morrow, 1994. (The chapter on the writing process has a strong section on writing conferences.)

Strunk, William, and E. B. White. *The Elements of Style*. Third edition. New York: Macmillan, 1979. (This reference is filled with revising and editing suggestions.)

Zinsser, William. *On Writing Well: An Informal Guide to Writing Nonfiction*. Third edition. New York: Harper and Row, 1985. (This classic has been expanded to cover writing with a word processor and organizing writing to prevent overwriting.)

Building Paragraphs

REFERENCES

Writing Paragraphs
Donald, Robert B., et al. *Writing Clear Paragraphs*. Englewood Cliffs: Prentice-Hall, 1978.

Writing a Summary
Irvin, Judith L. "Learning and Remembering." *Reading and the Middle School Student: Strategies to Enhance Literacy*. Boston: Allyn and Bacon, 1990.

RESOURCES

Kemper, Dave, Ruth Nathan, and Patrick Sebranek. *Writers Express: A Handbook for Young Writers, Thinkers, and Learners*. Lexington (MA): D.C. Heath, 1994. (This handbook for 4th and 5th graders includes many samples of paragraphs and summaries.)

Moffett, James. *Active Voices I*. Upper Montclair: Boynton Cook, 1987. (Contains many models of well-written paragraphs by children.)

Building Sentences

REFERENCES

Writing Basic Sentences
Petty, Walter T., Dorothy C. Petty, and Richard T. Salzer. "Supporting the Writing Process." *Experiences in Language*. Boston: Allyn and Bacon, 1994.

Combining Sentences
Strong, William. *Sentence Combining and Paragraph Building*. New York: McGraw, 1981.

RESOURCES

Killgallon, Don. *Sentence Composing: The Complete Course*. Portsmouth: Heinemann, 1987. (Offers practical sentence-building techniques.)

Moffett, James, and Betty Jane Wagner. *Student-Centered Language Arts, K-12*. Portsmouth: Heinemann, 1992. (Contains creative and thoughtful activities that help students develop their sentence sense.)

THE FORMS OF WRITING

Personal Writing

REFERENCES

Writing in Journals

Berthoff, Ann. "A Curious Triangle and the Double-Entry Notebook; or, How Theory Can Help Us Teach Reading and Writing." *The Making of Meaning: Metaphors, Models, and Maxims for Writing Teachers*. Portsmouth: Heinemann, 1981.

Halpern, Daniel, ed. "Journals, Notebooks, and Diaries." *Antaeus* Autumn 1988.

Kaye, Peggy. "Write a Letter." *Games for Writing*. New York: Farrar, Straus & Giroux, 1995.

Making Albums

Wilder, Laura Ingalls. *The Little House Book of Memories*. New York: Harper Collins Publishers, 1994.

Writing Lists

Ponsot, Marie, and Rosemary Deen. "Two-Part Essay Shapes: Coordinate Structures." *Beat Not the Poor Desk*. Portsmouth: Heinemann, 1982.

Writing Friendly Notes

Barkin, Carol, and Elizabeth James. *Sincerely Yours: How to Write Great Letters*. New York: Clarion, 1993.

Writing Friendly Letters

Barkin, Carol, and Elizabeth James. *Sincerely Yours: How to Write Great Letters*. New York: Clarion, 1993.

Writing Personal Narratives

Asher, Sandy. *Wild Words! How to Train Them to Tell Stories*. New York: Walker and Company, 1989.

Writing Family Stories

Buchman, Dian Dincin. *Family Fill-In Book: Discovering Your Roots*. New York: Scholastic, 1994.

Stillman, Peter. *Families Writing*. Cincinnati: Writer's Digest Books, 1989.

RESOURCES (listed on next page)

RESOURCES

Biffle, Christopher. *A Journey Through Your Childhood*. Los Angeles: Jeremy P. Tarcher, 1989. (This book helps teachers discover the power and pleasures of writing family stories.)

Cairney, Trevor. *Other Worlds: The Endless Possibilities of Literature*. Portsmouth: Heinemann, 1991. (Contains thematic units using literature, with specific procedures and follow-up activities. Includes a personal narrative unit.)

Fulwiler, Toby, ed. *The Journal Book*. Portsmouth: Heinemann, 1987. (In this book, theories, tips, and examples abound for all types of journal writing, at all different levels.)

Kaye, Peggy. "Make a List." *Games for Writing*. New York: Farrar, Straus & Giroux, 1995. (Gives a rationale and suggestions for list writing.)

Kaye, Peggy. "Write a Letter." *Games for Writing*. New York: Farrar, Straus & Giroux, 1995. (Helps young children write letters to people they don't know.)

Ohanian, Susan. "Making the Most of Simply Wonderful Lists." *Learning* Aug. 1985. (Uses lists from Dickens, Silverstein, and others to develop students' love of language.)

Ohanian, Susan. "Stacks of Letters" and "Love, Leslie." *Who's in Charge? A Teacher Speaks Her Mind*. Portsmouth: Heinemann, 1994. (Explains how to make letter exchanges a powerful classroom practice.)

Stevens, Carla. *A Book of Your Own: Keeping a Diary or Journal*. New York: Clarion Books, 1993. (Tells students everything they need to know to keep a journal.)

Subject Writing

REFERENCES

Writing Alphabet Books

Rosenberger, Francis Coleman. *An Alphabet.* Charlottesville: University Press of Virginia, 1978.

Writing Newspaper Stories

Clark, Roy Peter. *Free to Write: A Journalist Teaches Young Writers.* Portsmouth: Heinemann, 1987.

Writing Book Reviews

James, Elizabeth, and Carol Barkin. *How to Write Your Best Book Report.* New York: Lothrop, Lee & Shepard Books, 1986.

Writing Business Letters

United States Postal Service and the National Council of Teachers of English. *P.S. Write Soon! All About Letters.* Urbana: U.S. Postal Service and National Council of Teachers of English, 1982.

Writing to Explain

D'Arcy, Pat. "Writing to Explain." *Making Sense, Shaping Meaning.* Portsmouth: Heinemann, 1989.

RESOURCES

Granfield, Linda. *Extra! Extra! The Who, What, Where, When and Why of Newspapers.* New York: Orchard, 1993. (Gives step-by-step directions for creating a family, neighborhood, camp, or school newspaper.)

Hauser, Jill Frankel. *Kids' Crazy Concoctions: 50 Mysterious Mixtures for Art & Craft Fun.* Charlotte (VT): Williamson Publishing, 1995. (Contains many clearly written and playful how-to explanations.)

Moen, Christine Boardman. *Better Than Book Reports: More Than 40 Creative Responses to Literature.* New York: Scholastic, 1992. (Contains a collection of alternatives to the standard book review.)

Ohanian, Susan. "Across the Curriculum from A to Z." *Learning* Apr. 1987. (Includes resources and activities to help students think about, investigate, and enjoy words in every subject they study.)

Research Writing

REFERENCES

Using the Library
Hawes, Gene R., and Lynne Salop Hawes. *Hawes Guide to Successful Study Skills*. New York: New American Library, 1981.

Writing Classroom Reports
Doris, Ellen. *Doing What Scientists Do: Children Learn to Investigate Their World*. Portsmouth: Heinemann, 1991.

Grier, Katherine. *Discover: Investigate the Mysteries of History with 40 Practical Projects Probing Our Past*. Reading (MA): Royal Ontario Museum/Addison-Wesley, 1990.

James, Elizabeth, and Carol Barkin. *How to Write a Great School Report*. New York: Beech Tree Books, 1983.

Writing Photo Essays
Zarnowski, Myra. "Deciding and Documenting: Children Creating Portfolios." *Reading and Writing Nonfiction*. Schenectedy: New York State English Council, 1994.

RESOURCES

Moore, David, John Readence, and Robert Rickelman. "Graphically Representing Information." *Prereading Activities for Content Area Reading and Learning*. Second edition. Newark: International Reading Association, 1989. (Contains graphic organizers that also help students organize their factual writing.)

Ward, Geoff. *I've Got a Project On . . . .* Rozelle, Australia: PETA (Portsmouth: Heinemann, 1988). (Provides practical guidelines on every aspect of project development, from doing research to involving parents.)

Writing Stories, Tales, and Plays

REFERENCES

Writing Realistic Stories

Jenson, Julie M., and Nancy L. Roser, eds. *Adventuring with Books: A Booklist for Pre-K-Grade 6.* Tenth edition. Urbana: National Council of Teachers of English, 1993.

Moir, Hughes, ed. *Collected Perspectives: Choosing and Using Books for the Classroom.* Boston: Christopher-Gordon, 1992.

Roop, Peter, and Connie Roop. *Seasons of the Crane.* New York: Walker & Company, 1989.

Sutherland, Zena, and May Hill Arbuthnot. *Children and Books.* Eighth edition. New York: Harper Collins Publishers, 1991.

Writing Time-Travel Fantasies

Moss, Joy. *Focus Units in Literature: A Handbook for Elementary School Teachers.* Urbana: National Council of Teachers of English, 1984.

Writing Plays

Asher, Sandy. "The Elements of Play Writing." *Writers in the Classroom.* Ed. Ruth Nathan. Norwood (MA): Christopher-Gordon, 1991.

RESOURCES

Bishop, Rudine Sims, and the Multicultural Booklist Committee. *Kaleidoscope: A Multicultural Booklist for Grades K-8.* Urbana: National Council of Teachers of English, 1994. (This annotated list helps teachers find models of realistic fiction and fantasy across cultures.)

Cairney, Trevor H. "Today Was a Terrible Day." *Other Worlds: The Endless Possibilities of Literature.* Portsmouth: Heinemann, 1990. (The cited chapter is a literature unit using realistic fiction.)

Tarlington, Carole, and Patrick Verriour. *Role Drama.* Portsmouth: Heinemann, 1991. (This is a good introduction to performance of all kinds.)

Wood, Karen, and Anita Moss. "Making Drama with Literature." *Exploring Literature in the Classroom: Contents and Methods.* Norwood (MA): Christopher-Gordon, 1992. (The chapter explains using drama in the classroom for reflection on themes and issues.)

Writing Poems

REFERENCES

Writing Free-Verse Poetry and Writing Other Forms of Poetry

Cullinan, Bernice, et al. *Three Voices: An Invitation to Poetry Across the Curriculum.* York (ME): Stenhouse, 1995.

Denman, Gregory. *"When You've Made It Your Own . . ." Teaching Poetry to Young People.* Portsmouth: Heinemann, 1988.

Heard, Georgia. *For the Good of the Earth and Sun.* Portsmouth: Heinemann, 1989.

Janeczko, Paul. *Poetry from A to Z.* New York: Bradbury Press, 1994.

Moffett, James, and Betty Jane Wagner. *Student-Centered Language Arts and Reading, K-12.* Portsmouth: Heinemann, 1992.

Robb, Laura. *Whole Language, Whole Learners: Creating a Literature-Centered Classroom.* New York: William Morrow, 1994.

RESOURCES

Gensler, Kinereth, and Nina Nyhart. *The Poetry Connection: An Anthology of Contemporary Poems with Ideas to Stimulate Children's Writing.* New York: Teachers and Writers Collaborative, 1978. (Contains lessons followed by many models of children's poetry.)

Moir, Hughes, ed. *Collected Perspectives: Choosing and Using Books for the Classroom.* Boston: Christopher-Gordon, 1992. (Includes summaries of great children's literature with ways to use each entry in the classroom.)

Oliver, Mary. *A Poetry Handbook.* New York: Harcourt Brace and Co., 1994. (This is a beautiful, small handbook on writing poetry.)

Steinbergh, Judith. *Reading and Writing Poetry: A Guide for Teachers.* New York: Scholastic, 1994. (Provides lessons on listening to, learning about, reading, writing, and speaking poetry—very practical and easy to use.)

Williams, Miller. *Patterns of Poetry.* Baton Rouge: Louisiana State University Press, 1986. (This resource provides solid background knowledge about poetry.)

THE TOOLS OF LEARNING

Improving Your Reading

REFERENCES

Reading Graphics

Grant, E. A. *Kids' Book of Secret Codes, Signals, & Ciphers.* Philadelphia: Running Press, 1989.

The Visual Dictionary of the Earth. London: Dorling Kindersley, 1993.

Using Strategies to Read New Words

Cunningham, Patricia M., and Richard L. Allington. *Classrooms That Work: They Can All Read and Write.* New York: Harper Collins College Publishers, 1994.

Routman, Regie. *Transitions: From Literature to Literacy.* Portsmouth: Heinemann, 1988.

Reading to Understand

Cullinan, Bernice, ed. *Invitation to Read: More Children's Literature in the Reading Program.* Newark (DE): International Reading Association, 1992.

Daniels, Harvey. *Literature Circles: Voice and Choice in the Student-Centered Classroom.* York (ME): Stenhouse, 1995.

Herman, Beth Ann. *The Volunteer Tutor's Toolbox.* Newark (DE): International Reading Association, 1994.

Lang, Greg, and Chris Berberich. *All Children Are Special: Creating an Inclusive Classroom.* York (ME): Stenhouse, 1995.

Macrorie, Ken. "Foreword." *The Journal Book.* Portsmouth: Heinemann, 1988.

Ogle, Donna. "KWL: A Teaching Model That Develops Active Reading of Expository Text." *The Reading Teacher* 39.1 (1986).

Peterson, Ralph, and Maryann Eeds. *Grand Conversations: Literature Groups in Action.* New York: Scholastic, 1990.

Snow, Alan. *How Dogs Really Work!* Boston: Little, Brown and Company, 1993.

Tchudi, Stephen. *Sodapoppery.* New York: Charles Scribner's Sons, 1986.

Vergara, William. *Science in Everyday Life.* New York: Harper & Row, 1980.

RESOURCES

Macaulay, David. *The Way Things Work.* Boston: Houghton Mifflin Company, 1988. (Contains wonderful and often humorous diagrams of various machines and processes. Will help students understand diagrams.)

Powell, Debbie, and David Hornsby. *Learning Phonics and Spelling in a Whole Language Classroom.* New York: Scholastic, 1993. (Includes classroom-tested strategies, models, and activities to help students make graphophonic connections.)

Improving Vocabulary and Spelling

REFERENCES

Building Vocabulary Skills

Fry, Edward B. *New Reading Teacher's Book of Lists*. Englewood Cliffs: Prentice-Hall, 1985.

Nagy, William E. *Teaching Vocabulary to Improve Reading Comprehension*. Urbana: National Council of Teachers of English and International Reading Association, 1988.

Becoming a Better Speller

Graves, Donald. *Writing: Teachers and Children at Work*. Portsmouth: Heinemann, 1983.

Temple, Charles, and Jean Wallace Gillet. *Language Arts: Learning Processes and Teaching Practices*. Second edition. Glenview: Scott, Foresman and Company, 1989.

Temple, Charles, et al. *The Beginnings of Writing*. Third edition. Boston: Allyn and Bacon, 1993.

Wilde, Sandra. *You Kan Red This! Spelling and Punctuation for Whole Language Classrooms, K-6*. Portsmouth: Heinemann, 1992.

A History of the English Language

Pyles, Thomas. *The Origins and Development of the English Language*. Second edition. New York: Harcourt, 1971.

RESOURCES

Marzano, Robert, and Jana Marzano. *A Cluster Approach to Elementary Vocabulary Instruction*. Newark (DE): International Reading Association, 1988. (Discusses vocabulary building using superclusters of related words.)

Improving Speaking and Listening

REFERENCES

Learning to View
Barchers, Suzanne I. *Teaching Language Arts: An Integrated Approach*. St. Paul: West Publishing, 1994.

Learning to Listen
Barchers, Suzanne I. *Teaching Language Arts: An Integrated Approach*. St. Paul: West Publishing, 1994.

Performing Poems
Engler, Larry, and Carol Fijan. *Making Puppets Come Alive: A Method of Learning and Teaching Hand Puppetry*. New York: Taplinger Publishing Co., 1973.

Wolf, Allan. *It's Show Time: Poetry from the Page to the Stage*. Asheville: Poetry Alive! Publications, 1993.

Giving Short Talks
Moffett, James, and Betty Jane Wagner. *Student-Centered Language Arts, K-12*. Portsmouth: Heinemann, 1992.

Learning to Interview
Clark, Roy Peter. *Free to Write: A Journalist Teaches Young Writers*. Portsmouth: Heinemann, 1987.

Telling Stories
Hamilton, Martha, and Mitch Weiss. *Children Tell Stories*. Katonah (NY): Richard C. Owen Publishers, Inc., 1990.

Milord, Susan. *Tales Alive! Ten Multicultural Folktales with Activities*. Charlotte (VT): Williamson Publishing, 1995.

RESOURCES

Wolf, Allan. *Something Is Going to Happen*. Asheville: Iambic Publications, 1990. (This is a complete handbook for any K-college teacher interested in poetry performance.)

Yashinsky, Dan. *Next Teller: A Book of Canadian Storytelling*. Charlottetown (PEI, Canada): Ragweed Press, 1994. (Offers a marvelous collection of folktales about curious children, tricksters, hauntings, and more—perfect for telling.)

Improving Your Thinking

REFERENCES

Getting Organized

Armstrong, William H., and M. Willard Lampe II. *Study Tactics: A Master Plan for Success in School*. Woodbury (NY): Barron's, 1983.

Thinking Clearly

Udall, Anne J., and Joan E. Daniels. *Creating the Thoughtful Classroom: Strategies to Promote Student Thinking*. Tucson: Zephyr Press, 1991.

Writing to Learn Math

Burns, Marilyn. *A Collection of Math Lessons: From Grades 3 Through 6*. New Rochelle: Math Solution Publications, 1987.

RESOURCES

Burns, Marilyn. *About Teaching Mathematics: A K-8 Resource*. New Rochelle: Math Solutions Publications, 1992. (Presents a case for teaching math through problem solving and includes more than 240 classroom-tested activities.)

Golub, Jeffrey N. *Activities to Promote Critical Thinking*. Urbana: National Council of Teachers of English, 1986. (Twenty-eight teacher-tested activities help students think clearly and critically.)

Olson, Carol Booth. *Thinking Writing: Fostering Critical Thinking Through Writing*. New York: Harper Collins, 1992. (National Writing Project teachers offer strategies for integrating listening, speaking, reading, writing, and critical thinking across all grade levels.)

Improving Your Learning Skills

REFERENCES

Completing Assignments

Armstrong, William H., and M. Willard Lampe II. *Study Tactics: A Master Plan for Success in School*. Woodbury (NY): Barron's, 1983.

Working in Groups

Reid, Jo-Anne, Peter Forrestal, and Jonathan Cook. *Small Group Learning in the Classroom*. Toronto: Irwin Publishing, 1989.

Taking Tests

Armstrong, William H., and M. Willard Lampe II. *Study Tactics: A Master Plan for Success in School*. Woodbury (NY): Barron's, 1983.

Lorayne, Harry, and Jerry Lucas. *The Memory Book*. New York: Ballatine Books, 1974.

RESOURCES

Hawes, Gene R., and Lynne Salop Hawes. *Hawes Guide to Successful Study Skills*. New York: New American Library, 1981. (Contains good tips for completing assignments.)

Kesselmen-Turkel, Judi, and Franklynn Peterson. *Study Smarts: How to Learn More in Less Time*. Chicago: Contemporary Books, 1981. (This is a small informal book filled with tips on learning and remembering.)

THE STUDENT ALMANAC

REFERENCES

Using Maps

Reading Maps

Clouse, Nancy L. *Puzzle Maps U.S.A.* New York: Henry Holt, 1990.

VanCleaves, Janice. *Geography for Every Kid: Easy Activities That Make Learning Geography Fun*. New York: John Wiley & Sons, 1993.

Improving Math Skills

Solving Basic Word Problems

Burns, Marilyn. *A Collection of Math Lessons: From Grades 3 Through 6*. New Rochelle: Math Solution Publications, 1987.

Improving Handwriting

Graves, Donald. *Writing: Teachers and Children at Work*. Portsmouth: Heinemann, 1983.

History in the Making

Time Line

Grun, Bernard. *The Timetables of History: A Horizontal Linkage of People and Events*. New York: Touchstone/Simon & Schuster, Inc., 1979.

RESOURCES

Braddon, Kathryn L., et al., eds. *Math Through Children's Literature: Making the NCTM Standards Come Alive*. Englewood: Teacher Idea Press, 1993. (Connects literature to the National Council of Teachers of Mathematics standards.)

Burns, Marilyn. *About Teaching Mathematics: A K-8 Resource*. New Rochelle: Math Solution Publications, 1992. (Approaches math through problem solving and includes more than 240 classroom-tested activities.)

Griffiths, Rachel, and Margaret Clyne. *Books You Can Count On: Linking Mathematics and Literature*. Portsmouth: Heinemann, 1988. (Contains lesson outlines based on 40 different stories and poems.)

Pearl, Lila. *It Happened in America: True Stories from the Fifty States*. New York: Henry Holt, 1992. (Provides out-of-the-ordinary stories about each state.)

PLANNING NOTES

Reading/Writing Connections

RESOURCES

Calkins, Lucy McCormick. *The Art of Teaching Writing*. New edition. Portsmouth: Heinemann, 1994. (Responding to literature, writing to understand oneself and the world, and writing to reflect on one's own growth are just a few of the reading/writing connections Calkins explores.)

Hansen, Jane, et al., eds. *Breaking Ground: Teachers Relate Reading and Writing in the Elementary School*. Portsmouth: Heinemann, 1995. (Thirteen practicing teachers in language arts, social studies, and science and seven researchers in classrooms offer practical ways to combine reading and writing to help students learn.)

Jensen, Julie M., and Nancy L. Roser, eds. *Adventuring with Books*. Tenth edition. Urbana: National Council of Teachers of English, 1993. (Provides summaries of nearly 1,800 children's books published between 1988 and 1992.)

Kobrin, Beverly. *Eyeopeners II*. New York: Scholastic, 1995. (Lists 500 current nonfiction books; includes a helpful index organized by subject.)

Robb, Laura. *Whole Language, Whole Learners: Creating a Literature-Centered Classroom*. New York: William Morrow, 1994. (Fifteen essays on the creative process by some of today's best-known children's book authors make this book a must for teachers determined to broaden reading/writing connections.)

Routman, Regie. *Invitations: Changing as Teachers and Learners, K-12*. Portsmouth: Heinemann, 1991. (Contains 500 current nonfiction books; includes a helpful index organized by subject.)

Across-the-Curriculum Possibilities

RESOURCES

Atwell, Nancie, ed. *Coming to Know: Writing to Learn in the Intermediate Grades*. Portsmouth: Heinemann, 1990. (Explains procedures for report writing and ways to help children produce content-area writing that is as personal and meaningful as their own narratives.)

Fulwiler, Toby, ed. *The Journal Book*. Portsmouth: Heinemann, 1987. (Offers specific ways to begin and maintain writing across the curriculum using journals.)

Kucer, Stephen B., et al. *Curricular Conversations: Themes in Multilingual and Monolingual Classrooms*. York (ME): Stenhouse, 1995. (Outlines 29 themes, covering many interests and subjects. The reader will find specific organizational strategies for teachers in multilingual and monolingual classrooms.)

Tchudi, Stephen, ed. *The Astonishing Curriculum: Integrating Science and Humanities Through Language*. Urbana: National Council of Teachers of English, 1993. (Shows how astonishing curriculums are built from the questions and facts of students' lives.)

Students with Special Needs

RESOURCES

Berberich, Chris, and Greg Lang. *All Children Are Special*. York (ME): Stenhouse, 1995. (Provides strategies and techniques for nonspecialists who are teaching special-needs students in inclusive classrooms.)

Law, Barbara, and Mary Eckes. *The More Than Just Surviving Handbook: ESL for Every Classroom Teacher*. Winnipeg: Peguis, 1990. (Gives regular classroom teachers a place to start with ESL learners.)

Rhodes, Lynn K., and Curt Dudley-Marling. *Readers and Writers with a Difference: A Holistic Approach to Teaching Learning Disabled and Remedial Students*. Portsmouth: Heinemann, 1988. (Includes a chapter on observation and assessment.)

"Language Arts for 'Special Populations.'" *Language Arts* Nov. 1993. (Devoted to students with special needs and contains many models of students' work in the context of real classrooms.)

Assessment-Evaluation

RESOURCES

Anthony, Robert, et al. *Evaluating Literacy: A Perspective for Change*. Portsmouth: Heinemann, 1991. (This outstanding book on evaluation begins with the big picture and continues with a step-by-step approach to portfolio building. The sections "Me As a Student" and "My Work" are particularly helpful.)

Davies, Anne, et al. *Together Is Better: Collaborative Assessment, Evaluation, and Reporting*. Winnipeg: Peguis, 1992. (This is one of the finest books about three-way parent, teacher, and child assessing.)

Graves, Donald, and Bonnie Sustein. *Portfolio Portrait*. Portsmouth: Heinemann, 1992.

Jett-Simpson, Mary, and Lauren Leslie. *Ecological Assessment*. Schofield (WI): Wisconsin State Reading Association, 1994.

Potter, Shelly. *Portfolios and Student-Led Conferencing*. Birmingham (MI): Potter Press, 1992. (A small paperback with many blackline masters leading students to self-evaluation.)

Robb, Laura. *Whole Language, Whole Learners*. New York: William Morrow, 1994. (Contains a chapter on authentic assessment.)

Whitmore, Kathryn F., and Carol Crowell. *Inventing a Classroom: Life in a Bilingual, Whole Language Learning Community*. York (ME): Stenhouse, 1994. (Provides well-conceived whole language checklists in both English and Spanish plus a lively discussion of evaluation.)

PROGRAM Overview

This section provides an overview of the ***Write on Track Language Series***, the program of activities for grade 3 that coordinates with the student handbook. Of special interest to you will be the introduction to the *Language Series* on page 210 and the overview of activities that follows on pages 211-214. This section concludes with an explanation of various program activities from chapter notes to the two types of daily language sentences.

Building a Writing and Language Program with the *Write on Track Language Series*

The *Write on Track Language Series* is a complete language and learning program for level 3. The program provides teachers with a rich resource of activities—including, among other things, extended writing units, basic language units, practice workshops, minilessons, and MUG Shot Sentences for daily language practice. Other sections provide practical guidelines for implementing the program.

What is included in the series?

The Language Series is packaged in a program kit containing three basic elements. These elements include . . .

***Write on Track* Student Handbook**—A hardcover copy of the handbook is included for handy teacher reference. (Each student must have access to a copy of the student handbook as well.)

***Write on Track* Student SourceBook**—Each kit includes one SourceBook, containing workshops, minilessons, and MUG Shot Sentences for teachers to reproduce and use in their classrooms. (Classroom sets of the SourceBooks may also be purchased.)

The Program Guide—This three-ring binder contains more than 700 pages of information, including chapter notes and activities that coordinate with the chapters in the *Write on Track* handbook.

> **The overview charts on the next four pages identify the coordinating activities for each chapter in the student handbook.**

The PROCESS of Writing

	Type of Activity
Getting Started	
All About Writing	**Basic Unit**
One Writer's Process	**Basic Unit**
Writing with a Computer	**Basic Unit**
Planning Portfolios	**Basic Unit**
Publishing Your Writing	**Basic Unit**
Prewriting and Drafting Guide	
Building a File of Writing Ideas	**Basic Unit**
Collecting Details	**Basic Unit**
Planning and Drafting Guide	**Basic Unit**
Revising, Conferencing, and Editing Guide	
Revising Your Writing	**Basic Unit**
Conferencing with Partners	**Basic Unit**
Editing and Proofreading	**Basic Unit**
Building Paragraphs	
Writing Paragraphs	**Extended Unit**
Writing a Summary	**Extended Unit**
Building Sentences	
Writing Basic Sentences	**Basic Unit**
Combining Sentences	**Basic Unit**

The FORMS of Writing

	Type of Activity
Personal Writing	
Writing in Journals	**Basic Unit**
Making Albums	**Basic Unit**
Writing Lists	**Basic Unit**
Writing Friendly Notes	**Basic Unit**
Writing Friendly Letters	**Extended Unit**
Writing Personal Narratives	**Extended Unit**
Writing Family Stories	**Extended Unit**
Subject Writing	
Writing Alphabet Books	**Extended Unit**
Writing Newspaper Stories	**Extended Unit**
Writing Book Reviews	**Extended Unit**
Writing Business Letters	**Extended Unit**
Writing to Explain	**Extended Unit**
Research Writing	
Using the Library	**Extended Unit**
Writing Classroom Reports	**Extended Unit**
Writing Photo Essays	**Extended Unit**
Writing Stories, Tales, and Plays	
Writing Realistic Stories	**Extended Unit**
Writing Time-Travel Fantasies	**Extended Unit**
Writing Plays	**Extended Unit**
Writing Poems	
Writing Free-Verse Poetry	**Extended Unit**
Writing Other Forms of Poetry	**Extended Unit**

The **TOOLS** of Learning

The Proofreader's GUIDE

Type of Activity

Using Punctuation	
Checking Mechanics	
Checking Your Spelling	The basic skills in this section are covered in practice workshops, minilessons, and daily sentences.
Using the Right Word	
Understanding Sentences	
Understanding Our Language	

The Student ALMANAC

Useful Tables and Lists	**Basic Unit/Minilessons**
Using Maps	**Extended Unit**
Improving Math Skills	**Basic Unit**
Improving Handwriting	**Basic Unit/Minilessons**
History in the Making	**Basic Unit/Minilessons**

A Closer Look
at Chapter Notes

✳ **The chapter notes introduce you to each chapter in *Write on Track* and provide implementation guidelines and reproducible blackline masters.**

Writing to **Explain**
(pages 130-135)

Writing explanations will be a new experience for many third graders. But it is a form they will find increasingly useful (and important) as they advance in school. In a social studies class, they may be asked to explain how a certain part of government works; in science they may be asked to explain a process, and so on.

Writing to Explain, in the opening paragraph, makes an important point about this form—that some explanations help us *understand* things, and others help us *do* things. Also included on the introductory page is a fun set of directions for students to try. Complete guidelines for writing directions follow. The rest of the chapter contains a wonderful collection of model explanations.

Rationale
- Writing explanations helps students organize their thoughts.
- Writing explanations helps students sequence ideas and write clearly and precisely.
- Writing explanations has practical applications for students (giving directions, explaining experiments, and so on).

Major Concepts
- ✳ Explanations begin with a topic sentence (or a descriptive title), followed by clear, step-by-step directions. (pages 130-135)
- ✳ Action words (*put, stand, take*) tell the reader what to do. (pages 131, 133)
- ✳ Order words (*next, then, after*) help the reader follow each step. (page 131)

Materials Needed: Have a number of cookbooks for children on hand. Science and invention books describing various processes and how things work would also provide useful models.

Reading/Writing Connections: After reviewing the model explanations in the handbook, challenge students to find their own sample explanations in books and magazines. We recommend two books: *Bees Dance and Whales Sing* by Margery Facklam for its explanations of animal communication and *Creepy Cuisine* by Lucy Monroe for its precise recipe directions.

Across-the-Curriculum Possibilities: Writing explanations can obviously play an important role throughout the school curriculum. The introduction on this page suggests a few cross-curricular applications. You and your colleagues will think of many more.

Writing to Explain **65**

I. Introductory Page
Discusses the handbook chapter and provides planning notes

Getting Started (pages 130, 133-135)
- Begin by reading page 130 and the student models on pages 133-135. Choose one model to discuss further ("How to Get to My House from School" works well). As a class, talk about the importance of specific details. Encourage students to talk about what would happen if the writer had left out "front door" and just written "walk out of the school" instead. Also ask students to consider the importance of numbers (*two blocks, three houses*), relating them to accuracy and completeness.
- Have your students use the blackline master "I Know!" to think about and list ideas for their own written explanations.

Prewriting (page 131)
- Have students review the list of skills and talents they prepared on the "I Know!" master. Ask them to choose one especially interesting subject to write about step-by-step.
- Then give the students the blackline master "Step-by-Step." This activity will help students compile a list of the steps involved in explaining their subjects.

Writing the First Draft (page 131)
- Look over the student models on pages 133-135 again. With your students, pick out the subject of each model, the action words (*put, stand, take, punch, find, replace, watch*), order words (*first, next, finally*), and topic sentences (when applicable). Remind students that their own explanations will need to include these elements, too.
- Using the lists they have compiled in the prewriting activity, as well as the guidelines on handbook page 131, students should be ready to write their explanations. A blackline master, "Telling How to Do It," has been provided for this activity.

Revising, Editing, and Proofreading (page 132)
- Working in pairs, students should begin revising their first drafts. The blackline master "Checking It Twice" can be used as a checklist and then saved for future use. As always, remind students to check for misspelled words as well as for errors in punctuation and usage.
- After making corrections, they may write their final copies. Be sure to give students the chance to share their explanations with others. The real test is finding out whether or not someone else can follow a specific set of directions!

66 *Writing to Explain*

2. Write to the Handbook
Presents step-by-step implementation guidelines

Special Planning Notes

LESSON

Developing a set of directions as a class may help students better understand the process. Try the following topic: directions for visiting the library.

Write a topic sentence or appropriate title for this routine. Then, as a class, create a list of activities that are part of the library process. This list might include finding library books that are due, walking to the library, depositing books in the "book return," checking the card catalog to find books by a certain author or about a certain subject, finding these books, selecting one, checking it out, and returning to class.

Helping Students with Special Needs

Some students will find it easier to draw pictures of, rather than write about, the steps involved in an explanation. Let's say you ask them to explain how to locate information in the library. Before they begin their drawings, encourage students to talk about locating information in the library: *What do you do first? What do you do next?* Then give specific directions: *Draw three pictures to show how you use the library.* Now write a sentence or phrase for each picture. Finally, number the pictures in proper sequence.

Other Challenges

Have students (in pairs or in small groups) create a manual for doing something real or imagined. They could work on something serious like a manual for using the classroom computers. Or they could try something more imaginative, like the rules or directions for a made-up game. Encourage students to include colorful graphics in their manuals.

Writing to Explain **71**

3. Special Planning Notes
Offer additional planning ideas, including special-needs notes and other challenges

A Closer Look at Coordinating Blackline Masters

✳ The type and number of masters vary from chapter to chapter. The masters for most of "The Forms of Writing" chapters address different stages in the development of the students' writing.

Getting Started

Name _____

I Know!

Guess what! Like the students who wrote the models on pages 133-135 in the handbook, you have a talent for explaining things. And the better you know something, the easier it is for you to explain it.

DIRECTIONS: Read the four models in the handbook. Then brainstorm for all of the things you know. List your ideas in the blank spaces below. After you are done, put a star by one idea that really interests you.

I know how to make . . .   What I know how to do . . .

_____   _____
_____   _____
_____   _____

I can get to . . .   Here

_____
_____
_____

Prewriting

Name _____

Step-by-Step

DIRECTIONS: Write the name of your topic on the first line. Then list the steps in your explanation in the correct order. You do not have to use all the lines, and you do not have to write in complete sentences.

Here is what I will explain: _____

1. _____
2. _____
3. _____
4. _____
5. _____

Writing the First Draft

Name _____

Telling How to Do It

DIRECTIONS: Use the space below to write your first draft. Before you start, decide if you are going to list and number each step, or if you are going to write your directions in a paragraph. (If you write a paragraph, start with a topic sentence. If you list, be sure to number each step.)

Title _____

_____
_____
_____
_____
_____
_____
_____
_____
_____
_____

Writing to Explain **69**

Revising

Name _____

Checking It Twice

DIRECTIONS: Use the following checklist to help you review and revise your writing. These guidelines will help you check your classmates' work, too.

_____ 1. Make sure the topic sentence (or title if you've written a numbered list) names what you're explaining.

_____ 2. Make sure you have listed every step in your directions. Also make sure that your steps are in the right order.

_____ 3. Use complete sentences. (See page 70 in your handbook for a reminder about writing complete sentences.)

_____ 4. Use order words (*next, then, after*, . . .) to make the explanation easy to follow.

_____ 5. Check the action words (verbs). (For example, there is a big difference between "stir" and "beat" in cooking directions.)

70 *Writing to Explain*

A Closer Look at Practice Workshops

✳ More than 50 workshop activities are designed to provide advice, instruction, and practice related to basic writing and language skills.

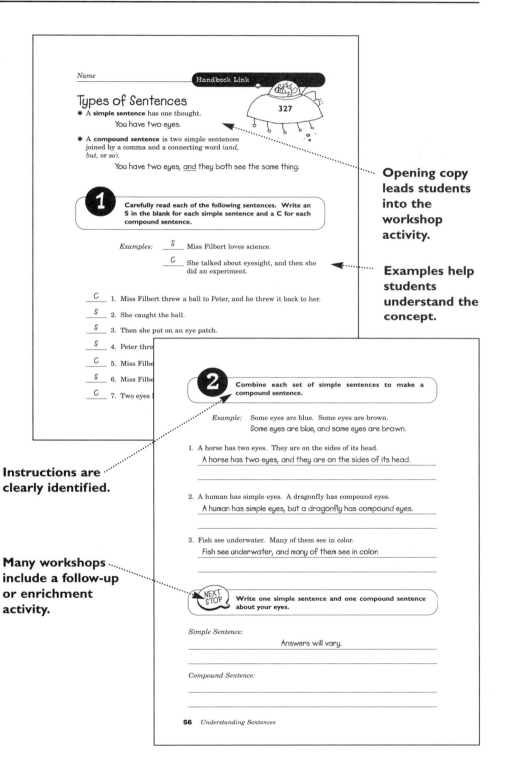

Opening copy leads students into the workshop activity.

Examples help students understand the concept.

Instructions are clearly identified.

Many workshops include a follow-up or enrichment activity.

Name _____

Handbook Link

Types of Sentences

✳ A **simple sentence** has one thought.
   You have two eyes.

✳ A **compound sentence** is two simple sentences joined by a comma and a connecting word (*and*, *but*, or *so*).
   You have two eyes, <u>and</u> they both see the same thing.

1 Carefully read each of the following sentences. Write an S in the blank for each simple sentence and a C for each compound sentence.

Examples: __*S*__ Miss Filbert loves science.

__*C*__ She talked about eyesight, and then she did an experiment.

__*C*__ 1. Miss Filbert threw a ball to Peter, and he threw it back to her.

__*S*__ 2. She caught the ball.

__*S*__ 3. Then she put on an eye patch.

__*S*__ 4. Peter thre

__*C*__ 5. Miss Filbe

__*S*__ 6. Miss Filbe

__*C*__ 7. Two eyes

2 Combine each set of simple sentences to make a compound sentence.

Example: Some eyes are blue. Some eyes are brown.
   Some eyes are blue, and some eyes are brown.

1. A horse has two eyes. They are on the sides of its head.
   A horse has two eyes, and they are on the sides of its head.

2. A human has simple eyes. A dragonfly has compound eyes.
   A human has simple eyes, but a dragonfly has compound eyes.

3. Fish see underwater. Many of them see in color.
   Fish see underwater, and many of them see in color.

NEXT STOP: Write one simple sentence and one compound sentence about your eyes.

Simple Sentence:
   Answers will vary.

Compound Sentence:

56 *Understanding Sentences*

A Closer Look at Minilessons

＊ More than 45 minilessons address usage, mechanics, and grammar skills covered in the handbook's "Proofreader's Guide" and other minilessons focus on information found in "The Student Almanac."

Opening copy leads students directly into the minilesson.

What is where? . . . . *Sentence Combining*

FILL IN the blanks in the sentences below. Use the map on page 354 of your handbook to help you. Then **COMBINE** each set of sentences into one sentence. (See page 73 in your handbook, "Combine with Compound Subjects.") The first one has been done for you.

Mississippi is near Florida.
Alabama is near Florida.

1. Georgia _____ is near Florida.

2. Mississippi, Alabama, and Georgia are near Florida. _____

Arizona is just north of Mexico.
New Mexico is just north of Mexico.

3. _____ is just north of Mexico.

4. _____

Montana is on Canada's border.
North Dakota on Canada's border.

5. _____ is on Canada's border.

6. _____

Washington is on the Pacific Ocean.
Oregon is on the Pacific Ocean.

7. _____ is on the Pacific Ocean.

8. _____

Some minilessons include examples to help students understand a concept.

Some minilessons can be reproduced as quick activity sheets.

118 *Understanding Sentences Minilessons*

A Closer Look at MUG Shot Sentences

✻ MUG Shot Sentences come in two varieties. In the focused sentences, students concentrate on one proofreading skill at a time. In the proofreading sentences, students address two or three different types of errors.

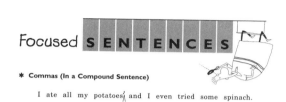

Focused SENTENCES

✻ **Commas (In a Compound Sentence)**

I ate all my potatoes‸ and I even tried some spinach.

✻ **Commas (In a Compound Sentence)**

My sister hid her lima beans‸ and our dog ate every one!

✻ **Commas (In a Compound Sentence)**

My dad took us to see a movie‸ but he didn't buy us any popcorn.

✻ **Commas (In a Compound Sentence)**

Joey invited me to his house‸ but I had too much homework to do.

✻ **Commas (In a Compou**

We could play b
rollerblading.

138 *MUG Shot Sentences*

Proofreading corrections can be placed in the original text.

Focused sentences are all clearly labeled with the same proofreading skill.

A title identifies the theme of the sentences on each page.

Proofreading SENTENCES

Greetings

✻ **Quotation Marks, Commas (To Set Off a Speaker's Words)**

"Bonjour‸" said the French visitor.

✻ **Quotation Marks, Commas (To Set Off a Speaker's Words)**

"Adios‸" called Juan as he walked away.

✻ **Using the Right Word, Capitalization**

I think ant Carla speaks Italian very well.

✻ **Capitalization, Titles**

Children can learn Spanish and English words while watching Sesame Street.

✻ **Using the Right Word, Capitalization**

Joe knows how to write sentences in English and Italian.

158 *MUG Shot Sentences*

Proofreading sentences are clearly labeled for the types of errors students will find.